Introduction

In 1904, *The Shame of the Cities* brought under one cover six magazine articles by Lincoln Steffens exposing the corruption of American municipal government. For more than half a century, the book has been famed an indispensable casebook for the practice of political reform.

But fame may tell us less about the quality of a book—or a man—than about the ethical appetite of the people who render homage. Clarification is sometimes necessary, a distinguishing between reputation and intrinsic merit.

In the fall of 1902, Steffens had been for a few months the managing editor of *McClure's Magazine*. Partly because of irritation arising from a confusion about editorial duties, partly because of S. S. McClure's irrepressible experimentalism, and chiefly because of Steffens' acknowledged reportorial skill, a decision was made to send the new man into the field. There is no evidence that anyone had much of an idea beyond looking into the news value of suspected prevalent corruption—with the obvious purpose of increasing the circulation of a new and ebullient magazine. There was no pretense at science, political or sociological. As Steffens says in his own Introduction to the book, the articles were "Done as journalism, they are journalism still."

The writer, however, was not without capacity; he was shrewd and brave, and was fully endowed with that moral indignation which inspired the Age of Reform.

In his review of the corruption of St. Louis, Minneapolis, Pittsburgh and Philadelphia, and the partial success of reform in Chicago and New York, Steffens named the givers and receivers of bribes, the vendors and buyers of privilege, and the managers and protectors of condoned criminality. He got from the honest prosecutors and other reform leaders the exact sums which changed hands and the place and time of payment, and all this was published to the nation at large. The factual survey in no way pretends to be complete, but the details presented were skillfully selected for drama and for power of impact.

In St. Louis, eighteen members of the municipal legislature were indicted, and the leaders are identified. We learn that in Minneapolis, when the corrupt "Doc Ames" came to power, 107 out of 225 policemen—probably the honest ones—were fired; and this account is followed by the name of a specific burglary planned by the men who were kept on the force. In Pittsburgh, paving contracts worth $3,517,731 went to the firm of the city's boss; $33,400 went to other companies; the favored contractor received from $1.00 to $1.80 more per square yard than the average in other cities. Newly appointed teachers in Philadelphia paid $120 out of their first $141 of salary to "the

262

The Shame of the Cities

Books by Lincoln Steffens

The Struggle for Self-Government
Upbuilders
Autobiography
The Least of These
Boy on Horseback

The Shame of

the Cities

BY LINCOLN STEFFENS

INTRODUCTION BY LOUIS JOUGHIN

AMERICAN CENTURY SERIES
HILL AND WANG · NEW YORK
A division of Farrar, Straus and Giroux

Standard Book Number: 8090-0008-3
Library of Congress Catalog Card Number: 57-9760

FIRST AMERICAN CENTURY SERIES EDITION 1957

Twenty-fourth printing, 1987

Manufactured in the United States of America

ring." Facts of this kind were bitter medicine to a nation that thought well of itself.

What did this evidence signify? In offering an explanation *The Shame of the Cities* is sometimes penetrating but is often fuzzy to the point of exasperation, at least for readers who have the perspective of another fifty years of American history.

The owner-publisher of the magazine had a controlling idea he wanted developed, at least at the start of the venture. Steffens, in the *Autobiography*, says "We had a pretty hot fight, and McClure won. What I went to Minneapolis to write was that democracy was a failure and that a good dictator was needed." Perhaps at the outset, and certainly as the articles were written, Steffens himself took the view that what was needed was an awakening of the people's conscience. Apparently he did not take McClure seriously: "The leading question raised in my second article on St. Louis was 'Is democracy a failure?' A trick, a political trick! I had no doubt that the people could and would govern themselves. . . ." But none of this really adds up to even a preliminary hypothesis of social corruption.

The articles, it is true, raise provocative questions. Steffens tells us that prosecuting attorney Joseph W. Folk in St. Louis regarded bribery as "no ordinary felony, but treason . . ." a view still entertained in some quarters. Steffens notes that "Public spirit became private spirit, public enterprise became private greed." The Pittsburgh ring is described as never breaking the law because it never had to; it simply rewrote the law to its purpose. Such remarks open the door to interesting speculation. But their author either plunges on to the next documented evil or merely reiterates his plea for civic conscience.

Another example. Steffens tells us that 20 out of 26

aldermen in Chicago with "bad records" were either denied nomination or defeated at the polls; this came about because the reform group successfully employed the techniques of practical politics to create an educated electorate. But there is no probing of the minds of the voters, and that, after all, was the field where evil met defeat.

Implicit in everything that Steffens wrote is a moral urgency. As Richard Hofstadter puts it in *The Age of Reform*, the chief appeal of the muckrakers was "not to desperate social needs but to mass sentiments of responsibility, indignation and guilt." For Steffens the clue to it all was a simple equation: "the corruption that shocks us in public affairs we practice in our private concerns. There is no essential difference between the pull that gets your wife into society or for your book a favorable review, and that which gets a heeler into office, a thief out of jail, and a rich man's son on the board of directors of a corporation; none between the corruption of a labor union, a bank, and a political machine. And it's all a moral weakness. The spirit of graft and of lawlessness is the American spirit."

This moral failure is constantly explained in terms of the dominance of our political life by business values: "The commercial spirit is the spirit of profit, not patriotism; of credit, not honor; of individual gain, not national prosperity; of trade and dickering, not principle . . . The typical business man is a bad citizen." Now whether this determination of guilt is correct is not the issue for an appraisal of the book; but what cannot be ignored is the fact that Steffens never comes to grips with his problem and offers no reasoning on a serious charge. The author of *The Shame of the Cities* was himself a cheerfully innocent buyer and seller of real estate and securities with a view to entirely honorable profit. And it is relevant to note the friendship between Steffens and Theodore Roosevelt, each man an amalgam of strenuous reform and innate conservatism.

Nevertheless, *The Shame of the Cities* is more than a testimonial to the insatiable appetite of Americans for virtue in all things—even government. The book's fame has at least two substantial grounds.

First, this classic of muckraking is a brave book. Steffens jests about the dangers he ran into in his investigations; actually he was in frequent contact with professional criminals whose vested interests were being mortally threatened. These men knew where Steffens stood and they might have quickly and brutally turned against him. But Steffens went ahead with his work; and courage, at least when it is augmented by intelligence, is not a quality to be discounted.

Second, the corruption Steffens exposed is not totally done with. Persons in government occasionally go to jail along with the men who bought them. The Pittsburgh system has come to life again in the curious form of legally guaranteed return to an ever-widening circle of business "allied with public interest," and indirectly to the employees of that kind of business.

Bravery, especially when the story is well told by a practitioner, will always engage our interest. A hard look at our social failures, unattenuated by cautious reservations or philosophy, warrants more than one reading. The final judgment on *The Shame of the Cities* may well be that it is the kind of book one cannot escape from. And there is always the good chance that it will move someone, a man like Steffens, to write it again for our time.

LOUIS JOUGHIN

New York City

Contents

Introduction; and Some Conclusions

This is not a book. It is a collection of articles reprinted from *McClure's Magazine*. Done as journalism, they are journalism still, and no further pretensions are set up for them in their new dress. This classification may seem pretentious enough; certainly it would if I should confess what claims I make for my profession. But no matter about that; I insist upon the journalism. And there is my justification for separating from the bound volumes of the magazine and republishing, practically without re-editing, my accounts as a reporter of the shame of American cities. They were written with a purpose, they were published serially with a purpose, and they are reprinted now together to further that same purpose, which was and is—to sound for the civic pride of an apparently shameless citizenship.

There must be such a thing, we reasoned. All our big boasting could not be empty vanity, nor our pious pretensions hollow sham. American achievements in science, art, and business mean sound abilities at bottom, and our hypocrisy a race sense of fundamental ethics. Even in government we have given proofs of potential greatness, and our political failures are not complete; they are simply ridiculous. But they are ours. Not alone the triumphs and the statesmen, the defeats and the grafters also represent us, and just as truly. Why not see it so and say it?

Because, I heard, the American people won't "stand for" it. You may blame the politicians, or, indeed, any one class, but not all classes, not the people. Or you may put it on the ignorant foreign immigrant, or any one nationality, but not on all nationalities, not on the American people. But no one class is at fault, nor any one breed, nor any particular interest or group of interests. The misgovernment of the American people is misgovernment by the American people.

When I set out on my travels, an honest New Yorker told me honestly that I would find that the Irish, the Catholic Irish, were at the bottom of it all everywhere. The first city I went to was St. Louis, a German city. The next was Minneapolis, a Scandinavian city, with a leadership of New Englanders. Then came Pittsburg, Scotch Presbyterian, and that was what my New York friend was. "Ah, but they are all foreign populations," I heard. The next city was Philadelphia, the purest American community of all, and the most hopeless. And after that came Chicago and New York, both mongrel-bred, but the one a triumph of reform, the other the best example of good government that I had seen. The "foreign element" excuse is one of the hypocritical lies that save us from the clear sight of ourselves.

Another such conceit of our egotism is that which deplores our politics and lauds our business. This is the wail of the typical American citizen. Now, the typical American citizen is the business man. The typical business man is a bad citizen; he is busy. If he is a "big business man" and very busy, he does not neglect, he is busy with politics, oh, very busy and very businesslike. I found him buying boodlers in St. Louis, defending grafters in Minneapolis, originating corruption in Pittsburg, sharing with bosses in Philadelphia, deploring reform in Chicago, and beating good government with corruption funds in New York. He is a self-righteous fraud, this big business man. He is the chief source of corruption, and it were a boon if he would neglect politics. But he is not the business man that neglects politics; that worthy is the good citizen, the typical business man. He too is busy, he is the one that has no use and therefore no time for politics. When his neglect has permitted bad government to go so far that he can be stirred to action, he is unhappy, and he looks around for a cure that shall be quick, so that he may hurry back to the shop. Naturally, too, when he talks politics, he talks shop. His patent remedy is quack; it is business.

"Give us a business man," he says ("like me," he means). "Let him introduce business methods into politics and government; then I shall be left alone to attend to my business."

There is hardly an office from United States Senator down to Alderman in any part of the country to which the business man has not been elected; yet politics remains corrupt, government pretty bad, and the selfish citizen has to hold himself in readiness like the old volunteer firemen to rush forth at any hour, in any weather, to prevent the fire; and he goes out sometimes and he puts out the fire (after the damage is done) and he goes back to the shop sighing for the business man in politics. The business man has failed in politics as he has in citizenship. Why?

Because politics is business. That's what's the matter with it. That's what's the matter with everything,—art, literature, religion, journalism, law, medicine,—they're all business, and all—as you see them. Make politics a sport, as they do in England, or a profession, as they do in Germany, and we'll have—well, something else than we have now,—if we want it, which is another question. But don't try to reform politics with the banker, the lawyer, and the dry-goods merchant, for these are business men and there are two great hindrances to their achievement of reform: one is that they are different from, but no better than, the politicians; the other is that politics is not "their line." There are exceptions both ways. Many politicians have gone out into business and done well (Tammany ex-mayors, and nearly all the old bosses of Philadelphia are prominent financiers in their cities), and business men have gone into politics and done well (Mark Hanna, for example). They haven't reformed their adopted trades, however, though they have sometimes sharpened them most pointedly. The politician is a business man with a specialty. When a business man of some other line learns the business of politics, he is a politician, and there is not much reform left in him. Consider the United States Senate, and believe me.

The commercial spirit is the spirit of profit, not patriotism; of credit, not honor; of individual gain, not national prosperity; of trade and dickering, not principle. "My business is sacred," says the business man in his heart. "Whatever prospers my business, is good; it must be. Whatever hinders it, is wrong; it must be. A bribe is bad, that is, it is a bad thing to take; but it is not so bad to give one, not if it is necessary to my business." "Business is business" is not a political sentiment, but our politician has caught it. He takes essentially the same view of the bribe, only he saves his self-respect by piling all his contempt upon the bribe-giver, and he has the great advantage of candor. "It is wrong, maybe," he says, "but if a rich merchant can afford to do business with me for the sake of a convenience or to increase his already great wealth, I can afford, for the sake of a living, to meet him half way. I make no pretensions to virtue, not even on Sunday." And as for giving bad government or good, how about the merchant who gives bad goods or good goods, according to the demand?

But there is hope, not alone despair, in the commercialism of our politics. If our political leaders are to be always a lot of political merchants, they will supply any demand we may create. All we have to do is to establish a steady demand for good government. The bosses have us split up into parties. To him parties are nothing but means to his corrupt ends. He "bolts" his party, but we must not; the bribe-giver changes his party, from one election to another, from one county to another, from one city to another, but the honest voter must not. Why? Because if the honest voter cared no more for his party than the politician and the grafter, then the honest vote would govern, and that would be bad—for graft. It is idiotic, this devotion to a machine that is used to take our sovereignty from us. If we would leave parties to the politicians, and would vote not for the party, not even for men, but for the city, and the State, and the nation, we should rule parties, and cities, and States, and nation. If we would vote in mass on the more promising ticket, or, if the two are equally bad, would throw out the party that is in, and wait till the next election and then throw out the other party that is in—then, I say, the commercial politician would feel a demand for good government and he would supply it. That process would take a generation or more to complete, for the politicians now really do not know what good government is. But it has taken as long to develop bad government, and the politicians know what that is. If it would not "go," they would offer something else, and, if the demand were steady, they, being so commercial, would "deliver the goods."

But do the people want good government? Tammany says they don't. Are the people honest? Are the people better than Tammany? Are they better than the merchant and the politician? Isn't our corrupt government, after all, representative?

President Roosevelt has been sneered at for going about the country preaching, as a cure for our American evils, good conduct in the individual, simple honesty, courage, and efficiency. "Platitudes!" the sophisticated say. Platitudes? If my observations have been true, the literal adoption of Mr. Roosevelt's reform scheme would result in a revolution, more radical and terrible to existing institutions, from the Congress to the Church, from the bank to the ward organization, than socialism or even than anarchy. Why, that would change all of us—not alone our neighbors, not alone the grafters, but you and me.

No, the contemned methods of our despised politics

are the master methods of our braggart business, and the corruption that shocks us in public affairs we practice ourselves in our private concerns. There is no essential difference between the pull that gets your wife into society or for your book a favorable review, and that which gets a heeler into office, a thief out of jail, and a rich man's son on the board of directors of a corporation; none between the corruption of a labor union, a bank, and a political machine; none between a dummy director of a trust and the caucus-bound member of a legislature; none between a labor boss like Sam Parks, a boss of banks like John D. Rockefeller, a boss of railroads like J. P. Morgan, and a political boss like Matthew S. Quay. The boss is not a political, he is an American institution, the product of a freed people that have not the spirit to be free.

And it's all a moral weakness; a weakness right where we think we are strongest. Oh, we are good—on Sunday, and we are "fearfully patriotic" on the Fourth of July. But the bribe we pay to the janitor to prefer our interests to the landlord's, is the little brother of the bribe passed to the alderman to sell a city street, and the father of the air-brake stock assigned to the president of a railroad to have this life-saving invention adopted on his road. And as for graft, railroad passes, saloon and bawdy-house blackmail, and watered stock, all these belong to the same family. We are pathetically proud of our democratic institutions and our republican form of government, of our grand Constitution and our just laws. We are a free and sovereign people, we govern ourselves and the government is ours. But that is the point. We are responsible, not our leaders, since we follow them. We *let* them divert our loyalty from the United States to some "party"; we *let* them boss the party and turn our municipal democracies into autocracies and our republican nation into a plutocracy. We cheat our government and we let our leaders loot it, and we let them wheedle and bribe our sovereignty from us. True, they pass for us strict laws, but we are content to let them pass also bad laws, giving away public property in exchange; and our good, and often impossible, laws we allow to be used for oppression and blackmail. And what can we say? We break our own laws and rob our own government, the lady at the customhouse, the lyncher with his rope, and the captain of industry with his bribe and his rebate. The spirit of graft and of lawlessness is the American spirit.

And this shall not be said? Not plainly? William Travers Jerome, the fearless District Attorney of New York, says, "You can say anything you think to the American people. If you are honest with yourself you may be honest with them, and they will forgive not only your candor, but your mistakes." This is the opinion, and the experience too, of an honest man and a hopeful democrat. Who says the other things? Who says "Hush," and "What's the use?" and "ALL's well," when all is rotten? It is the grafter; the coward, too, but the grafter inspires the coward. The doctrine of "addition, division, and silence" is the doctrine of graft. "Don't hurt the party," "Spare the fair fame of the city," are boodle yells. The Fourth of July oration is the "front" of graft. There is no patriotism in it, but treason. It is part of the game. The grafters call for cheers for the flag, "prosperity," and "the party," just as a highway man commands "hands up," and while we are waving and shouting, they float the flag from the nation to the party, turn both into graft factories, and prosperity into a speculative boom to make "weak hands," as the Wall Street phrase has it, hold the watered stock while the strong hands keep the property. "Blame us, blame anybody, but praise the people," this, the politician's advice, is not the counsel of respect for the people, but of contempt. By just such palavering as courtiers play upon the degenerate intellects of weak kings, the bosses, political, financial, and industrial, are befuddling and befooling our sovereign American citizenship; and—likewise—they are corrupting it.

And it is corruptible, this citizenship. "I know what Parks is doing," said a New York union workman, "but what do I care. He has raised my wages. Let him have his graft!" And the Philadelphia merchant says the same thing: "The party leaders may be getting more than they should out of the city, but that doesn't hurt me. It may raise taxes a little, but I can stand that. The party keeps up the protective tariff. If that were cut down, my business would be ruined. So long as the party stands pat on that, I stand pat on the party."

The people are not innocent. That is the only "news" in all the journalism of these articles, and no doubt that was not new to many observers. It was to me. When I set out to describe the corrupt systems of certain typical cities, I meant to show simply how the people were deceived and betrayed. But in the very first study—St. Louis—the startling truth lay bare that corruption was not merely political; it was financial, commercial, social; the ramifications of boodle were so complex, various, and far-reaching, that one mind could hardly grasp them, and not even Joseph W. Folk, the tireless prosecutor, could follow them all. This state of things was indicated in the first article which Claude H. Wetmore and I compiled together, but it was not shown plainly enough. Mr. Wetmore lived in St. Louis, and he had respect for names which meant little to me. But when I went next to Minneapolis alone, I could see more independently, without respect for persons, and there were traces of the same phenomenon. The first St. Louis article was called "Tweed Days in St. Louis," and though the "better citizen" received attention the Tweeds were the center of interest. In "The Shame of Minneapolis," the truth was put into the title; it was the Shame of Minneapolis; not of the Ames administration, not of the Tweeds, but of the city and its citizens. And yet Minneapolis was not nearly so bad as St. Louis; police graft is never so universal as boodle. It is more shocking, but it is so filthy that it cannot involve so large a part of society. So I returned to St. Louis, and I went over the whole ground again, with the people in mind, not alone the caught and convicted boodlers. And this time the true meaning of "Tweed Days in St. Louis" was made plain. The article was called "The Shamelessness of St. Louis," and that was the burden of the story. In Pittsburg also the people was the subject, and though the civic spirit there was better, the extent of the corruption throughout the social organization of the community was indicated. But it was not till I got to Philadelphia that the possibilities of popular corruption were worked out to the limit of humiliating confession. That was the place for such a study. There is nothing like it in the country, except possibly, in Cincinnati. Philadelphia certainly is not merely corrupt, but corrupted, and this was made clear. Philadelphia was charged up to—the American citizen.

It was impossible in the space of a magazine article to cover in any one city all the phases of municipal government, so I chose cities that typified most strikingly some particular phase or phases. Thus as St. Louis exemplified boodle; Minneapolis, police graft; Pittsburg, a political and industrial machine; and Philadelphia, general civic corruption; so Chicago was an illustration of reform, and New York of good government. All these things occur in most of these places. There are, and long have been, reformers in St. Louis, and there is to-day police graft there. Minneapolis has had boodling and council reform, and boodling is breaking out there again. Pittsburg has general corruption, and Philadelphia a very perfect political machine. Chicago has police graft and a low order of administrative and general corruption which permeates business, labor, and society generally. As for New York, the metropolis might exemplify almost anything that occurs anywhere in American cities, but no city has had for many years such a good administration as was that of Mayor Seth Low.

That which I have made each city stand for, is that which it had most highly developed. It would be absurd to seek for organized reform in St. Louis, for example, with Chicago next door; or for graft in Chicago with Minneapolis so near. After Minneapolis, a description of administrative corruption in Chicago would have seemed like a repetition. Perhaps it was not just to treat only the conspicuous element in each situation. But why should I be just? I was not judging; I arrogated to myself no such function. I was not writing about Chicago for Chicago, but for the other cities, so I picked out what light each had for the instruction of the others. But, if I was never complete, I never exaggerated. Every one of those articles was an understatement, especially where the conditions were bad, and the proof thereof is that while each article seemed to astonish other cities, it disappointed the city which was its subject. Thus my friends in Philadelphia, who knew what there was to know, and those especially who knew what I knew, expressed surprise that I reported so little. And one St. Louis newspaper said that "the facts were thrown at me and I fell down over them." There was truth in these flings. I cut twenty thousand words out of the Philadelphia article and then had not written half my facts. I know a man who is making a history of the corrupt construction of the Philadelphia City Hall, in three volumes, and he grieves because he lacks space. You can't put all the known incidents of the corruption of an American city into a book.

This is all very unscientific, but then, I am not a scientist. I am a journalist. I did not gather with indifference all the facts and arrange them patiently for permanent preservation and laboratory analysis. I did not want to preserve, I wanted to destroy the facts. My purpose was no more scientific than the spirit of my investigation and reports; it was, as I said above, to see if the shameful facts, spread out in all their shame, would not burn through our civic shamelessness and set fire to American pride. That was the journalism of it. I wanted to move and to convince. That is why I was not interested in all the facts, sought none that was new, and rejected half those that were old. I often was asked to expose something suspected. I couldn't; and why should I? Exposure of the unknown was not my purpose. The people: what they will put up with, how they are fooled, how cheaply they are bought, how dearly sold, how easily intimidated, and how led, for good or for evil—that was the inquiry, and so the significant facts were those only which everybody in each city knew, and of these, only those which everybody in every other town would recognize, from their common knowledge of such things, to be probable. But these, understated, were charged always to the guilty persons when individuals were to blame, and finally brought home to the people themselves, who, having the power, have also the responsibility, they and those they respect, and those that guide them.

This was against all the warnings and rules of demagogy. What was the result?

After Joseph W. Folk had explored and exposed, with convictions, the boodling of St. Louis, the rings carried an election. "Tweed Days in St. Louis" is said to have formed some public sentiment against the boodlers, but the local newspapers had more to do with that than *McClure's Magazine*. After the Minneapolis grand jury had exposed and the courts had tried and the common juries had convicted the grafters there, an election showed that public opinion was formed. But that one election was regarded as final. When I went there the men who had led the reform movement were "all through." After they had read the "Shame of Minneapolis," however, they went back to work, and they have perfected a plan to keep the citizens informed and to continue the fight for good government. They saw, these unambitious, busy citizens, that it was "up to them," and they resumed the unwelcome duties of their citizenship. Of resentment there was very little. At a meeting of leading citizens there were honest speeches suggesting that something should be said to "clear the name of Minneapolis," but one man rose and said very pleasantly, but firmly, that the article was true; it was pretty hard on them, but it was true and they all knew it. That ended that.

When I returned to St. Louis and rewrote the facts, and, in rewriting, made them just as insulting as the truth would permit, my friends there expressed dismay over the manuscript. The article would hurt Mr. Folk; it would hurt the cause; it would arouse popular wrath.

"That was what I hoped it would do," I said.

"But the indignation would break upon Folk and reform, not on the boodlers," they said.

"Wasn't it obvious," I asked, "that this very title, 'Shamelessness,' was aimed at pride; that it implied a faith that there was self-respect to be touched and shame to be moved?"

That was too subtle. So I answered that if they had no faith in the town, I had, and anyway, if I was wrong and the people should resent, not the crime, but the exposure of it, then they would punish, not Mr. Folk, who had nothing to do with the article, but the magazine and me. Newspaper men warned me that they would not "stand for" the article, but would attack it. I answered that I would let the St. Louisans decide between us. It was true, it was just; the people of St. Louis had shown no shame. Here was a good chance to see whether they had any. I was a fool, they said. "All right," I replied. "All kings had fools in the olden days, and the fools were allowed to tell them the truth. I would play the fool to the American people."

The article, published, was attacked by the newspapers; friends of Mr. Folk repudiated it; Mr. Folk himself spoke up for the people. Leading citizens raised money for a mass meeting to "set the city right before the world." The mayor of the city, a most excellent man, who had helped me, denounced the article. The boodle party platform appealed for votes on the strength of the attacks in "Eastern magazines." The people themselves contradicted me; after the publication, two hundred thousand buttons for "Folk and Reform" were worn on the streets of St. Louis.

But those buttons were for "Folk and Reform." They did go to prove that the article was wrong, that there was pride in St. Louis, but they proved also that that pride had been touched. Up to that time nobody knew exactly how St. Louis felt about it all. There had been one election, another was pending, and the boodlers, caught or to be caught, were in control. The citizens had made no move to dislodge them. Mr. Folk's splendid labors were a spectacle without a chorus, and, though I had met men who told me the people were with Folk, I had met also the grafters, who cursed only Folk and were building all their hopes on the assumption that "after Folk's term" all would be well again. Between these two local views no outsider could choose. How could I read a strange people's hearts? I took the outside view, stated the facts both ways, —the right verdicts of the juries and the confident plans of the boodlers,—and the result was, indeed, a shameless state of affairs for which St. Louis, the people of St. Louis, were to blame.

And they saw it so, both in the city and in the State, and they ceased to be spectators. That article simply got down to the self-respect of this people. And who was hurt? Not St. Louis. From that moment the city has been determined and active, and boodle seems to be doomed. Not Mr. Folk. After that, his nomination for Governor of the State was declared for by the people, who formed Folk clubs all over the State to force him upon his party and theirs, and thus insure the pursuit of the boodlers in St. Louis and in Missouri too. Nor was the magazine hurt, or myself. The next time I went to St. Louis, the very men who had raised money for the mass meeting to denounce the article went out of their way to say to me that I had been right, the article was true, and they asked me to "do it again." And there may be a chance to do it again. Mr. Folk lifted the lid off Missouri for a moment after that, and the State also appeared ripe for the gathering. Moreover, the boodlers of State and city have joined to beat the people and keep them down. The decisive election is not till the fall of 1904, and the boodlers count much on the fickleness of public opinion. But I believe that Missouri and St. Louis together will prove then, once for all, that the people can rule—when they are aroused.

The Pittsburg article had no effect in Pittsburg, nor had that on Philadelphia any results in Philadelphia. Nor was any expected there. Pittsburg, as I said in the article, knew itself, and may pull out of its disgrace, but Philadelphia is contented and seems hopeless. The accounts of them, however, and indeed, as I have said, all of the series, were written, not for the cities described, but for all our cities; and the most immediate response came from places not mentioned, but where similar evils existed or similar action was needed. Thus Chicago, intent on its troubles, found useless to it the study of its reform, which seems to have been suggestive elsewhere, and Philadelphia, "Corrupt and Contented," was taken home in other cities and seems to have made the most lasting impression everywhere.

But of course the tangible results are few. The real triumph of the year's work was the complete demonstration it has given, in a thousand little ways, that our shamelessness is superficial, that beneath it lies a pride which, being real, may save us yet. And it is real. The grafters who said you may put the blame anywhere but on the people, where it belongs, and that Americans can be moved only by flattery,—they lied. They lied about themselves. They, too, are American citizens; they too, are of the people; and some of them also were reached by shame. The great truth I tried to make plain was that which Mr. Folk insists so constantly upon: that bribery is no ordinary felony, but treason, that the "corruption which breaks out here and there and now and then" is not an occasional offense, but a common practice, and that the effect of it is literally to change the form of our government from one that is representative of the people to an oligarchy, representative of special interests. Some politicians have seen that this is so, and it bothers them. I think I prize more highly than any other of my experiences the half-dozen times when grafting politicians I had "roasted," as they put it, called on me afterwards to say, in the words of one who spoke with a wonderful solemnity:

"You are right. I never thought of it that way, but it's right. I don't know whether you can do anything, but you're right, dead right. And I'm all wrong. We're all, all wrong. I don't see how we can stop it now; I don't see how I can change. I can't, I guess. No, I can't, not now. But, say, I may be able to help you, and I will if I can. You can have anything I've got."

So you see, they are not such bad fellows, these practical politicians. I wish I could tell more about them: how they have helped me; how candidly and unselfishly they have assisted me to facts and an understanding of the facts, which, as I warned them, as they knew well, were to be used against them. If I could—and I will some day —I should show that one of the surest hopes we have is the politician himself. Ask him for good politics; punish him when he gives bad, and reward him when he gives good; make politics pay. Now, he says, you don't know and you don't care, and that you must be flattered and fooled—and there, I say, he is wrong. I did not flatter anybody; I told the truth as near as I could get it, and instead of resentment there was encouragement. After "The Shame of Minneapolis," and "The Shamelessness of St. Louis," not only did citizens of these cities approve, but citizens of other cities, individuals, groups, and organizations, sent in invitations, hundreds of them, "to come and show us up; we're worse than they are."

We Americans may have failed. We may be mercenary and selfish. Democracy with us may be impossible and corruption inevitable, but these articles, if they have proved nothing else, have demonstrated beyond doubt that we can stand the truth; that there is pride in the character of American citizenship; and that this pride may be a power in the land. So this little volume, a record of shame and yet of self-respect, a disgraceful confession, yet a declaration of honor, is dedicated, in all good faith, to the accused—to all the citizens of all the cities in the United States.

New York, December, 1903

Tweed Days in St. Louis

(*October, 1902*)

St. Louis, the fourth city in size in the United States, is making two announcements to the world: one that it is the worst-governed city in the land; the other that it wishes all men to come there (for the World's Fair) and see it. It isn't our worst-governed city; Philadelphia is that. But St. Louis is worth examining while we have it inside out.

There is a man at work there, one man, working all alone, but he is the Circuit (district or State) Attorney, and he is "doing his duty." That is what thousands of district attorneys and other public officials have promised to do and boasted of doing. This man has a literal sort of mind. He is a thin-lipped, firm-mouthed, dark little man, who never raises his voice, but goes ahead doing, with a smiling eye and a set jaw, the simple thing he said he would do. The politicians and reputable citizens who asked him to run urged him when he declined. When he said that if elected he would have to do his duty, they said, "Of course." So he ran, they supported him, and he was elected. Now some of these politicians are sentenced to the penitentiary, some are in Mexico. The Circuit Attorney, finding that his "duty" was to catch and convict criminals, and that the biggest criminals were some of these same politicians and leading citizens, went after them. It is magnificent, but the politicians declare it isn't politics.

The corruption of St. Louis came from the top. The best citizens—the merchants and big financiers—used to rule the town, and they ruled it well. They set out to outstrip Chicago. The commercial and industrial war between these two cities was at one time a picturesque and dramatic spectacle such as is witnessed only in our country. Business men were not mere merchants and the politicians were not mere grafters; the two kinds of citizens got together and wielded the power of banks, railroads, factories, the prestige of the city, and the spirit of its citizens to gain business and population. And it was a close race. Chicago, having the start, always led, but St. Louis had pluck, intelligence, and tremendous energy. It pressed Chicago hard. It excelled in a sense of civic beauty and good government; and there are those who think yet it might have won. But a change occurred. Public spirit became private spirit, public enterprise became private greed.

Along about 1890, public franchises and privileges were sought, not only for legitimate profit and common convenience, but for loot. Taking but slight and always selfish interest in the public councils, the big men misused politics. The riffraff, catching the smell of corruption, rushed into the Municipal Assembly, drove out the remaining respectable men, and sold the city—its streets, its wharves, its markets, and all that it had—to the now greedy business men and bribers. In other words, when the leading men began to devour their own city, the herd rushed into the trough and fed also.

So gradually has this occurred that these same citizens hardly realize it. Go to St. Louis and you will find the habit of civic pride in them; they still boast. The visitor is told of the wealth of the residents, of the financial strength of the banks, and of the growing importance of the industries, yet he sees poorly paved, refuse-burdened streets, and dusty or mud-covered alleys; he passes a ramshackle fire-trap crowded with the sick, and learns that it is the City Hospital; he enters the "Four Courts," and his nostrils are greeted by the odor of formaldehyde used as a disinfectant, and insect powder spread to destroy vermin; he calls at the new City Hall, and finds half the entrance boarded with pine planks to cover up the unfinished interior. Finally, he turns a tap in the hotel, to see liquid mud flow into wash-basin or bath-tub.

The St. Louis charter vests legislative power of great scope in a Municipal Assembly, which is composed of a council and a House of Delegates. Here is a description of the latter by one of Mr. Folk's grand juries:

"We have had before us many of those who have been, and most of those who are now, members of the House of Delegates. We found a number of these utterly illiterate and lacking in ordinary intelligence, unable to give a better reason for favoring or opposing a measure than a desire to act with the majority. In some, no trace of mentality or morality could be found; in others, a low order of training appeared, united with base cunning, groveling instincts, and sordid desires. Unqualified to respond to the ordinary requirements of life, they are utterly incapable of comprehending the significance of an ordinance, and are incapacitated, both by nature and training, to be the makers of laws. The choosing of such men to be legislators makes a travesty of justice, sets a premium on incompetency, and deliberately poisons the very source of the law."

These creatures were well organized. They had a "combine"—a legislative institution—which the grand jury described as follows:

"Our investigation, covering more or less fully a period of ten years, shows that, with few exceptions, no ordinance has been passed wherein valuable privileges or franchises are granted until those interested have paid the legislators the money demanded for action in the particular case. Combines in both branches of the Municipal Assembly are formed by members sufficient in number to control legislation. To one member of this combine is delegated the authority to act for the combine, and to receive and to distribute to each member the money agreed upon as the price of his vote in support of, or opposition to, a pending measure. So long has this practice existed that such members have come to regard the receipt of money for action on pending measures as a legitimate perquisite of a legislator."

One legislator consulted a lawyer with the intention of suing a firm to recover an unpaid balance on a fee for the grant of a switch-way. Such difficulties rarely occurred, however. In order to insure a regular and indisputable revenue, the combine of each house drew up a schedule of bribery prices for all possible sorts of grants, just such a list as a commercial traveler takes out on the road with him. There was a price for a grain elevator, a price for a short switch; side tracks were charged for by the linear foot, but at rates which varied according to the nature of the ground taken; a street improvement cost so much; wharf space was classified and precisely rated. As there was a scale for favorable legislation, so there was one for defeating bills. It made a difference in the price if there was opposition, and it made a difference whether the privilege asked was legitimate or not. But nothing was passed free of charge. Many of the legislators were saloon-keepers—it was in St. Louis that a practical joker nearly emptied the House of Delegates by tipping a boy to rush into a session and call out, "Mister, your saloon is on fire,"—but even the saloon-keepers of a neighborhood had to pay to keep in their inconvenient locality a market which public interest would have moved.

From the Assembly, bribery spread into other departments. Men empowered to issue peddlers' licenses and permits to citizens who wished to erect awnings or use a portion of the sidewalk for storage purposes charged an amount in excess of the prices stipulated by law, and pocketed the difference. The city's money was loaned at interest, and the interest was converted into private bank accounts. City carriages were used by the wives and children of city officials. Supplies for public institutions found their way to private tables; one itemized account of food furnished the poorhouse included California jellies, imported cheeses, and French wines! A member of the Assembly caused the incorporation of a grocery company, with his sons and daughters the ostensible stockholders, and succeeded in having his bid for city supplies accepted although the figures were in excess of his competitors'. In return for the favor thus shown, he indorsed a measure to award the contract for city printing to another member, and these two voted aye on a bill granting to a third the exclusive right to furnish city dispensaries with drugs.

Men ran into debt to the extent of thousands of dollars for the sake of election to either branch of the Assembly. One night, on a street car going to the City Hall, a new member remarked that the nickel he handed the conductor was his last. The next day he deposited $5,000 in a savings bank. A member of the House of Delegates admitted to the Grand Jury that his dividends from the combine netted $25,000 in one year; a Councilman stated that he was paid $50,000 for his vote on a single measure.

Bribery was a joke. A newspaper reporter overheard this conversation one evening in the corridor of the City Hall:

"Ah there, my boodler!" said Mr. Delegate.

"Stay there, my grafter!" replied Mr. Councilman. "Can you lend me a hundred for a day or two?"

"Not at present. But I can spare it if the Z—— bill goes through to-night. Meet me at F——'s later."

"All right, my jailbird; I'll be there."

The blackest years were 1898, 1899, and 1900. Foreign corporations came into the city to share in its despoliation, and home industries were driven out by blackmail. Franchises worth millions were granted without one cent of cash to the city, and with provision for only the smallest future payment; several companies which refused to pay blackmail had to leave; citizens were robbed more and more boldly; pay-rolls were padded with the names of non-existent persons; work on public improvements was neglected, while money for them went to the boodlers.

Some of the newspapers protested, disinterested citizens were alarmed, and the shrewder men gave warnings, but none dared make an effective stand. Behind the corruptionists were men of wealth and social standing, who, because of special privileges granted them, felt bound to support and defend the looters. Independent victims of the far-reaching conspiracy submitted in silence, through fear of injury to their business. Men whose integrity was never questioned, who held high positions of trust, who were church members and teachers of Bible classes, contributed to the support of the dynasty, —became blackmailers, in fact,—and their excuse was that others did the same, and that if they proved the exception it would work their ruin. The system became loose through license and plenty till it was as wild and weak as that of Tweed in New York.

Then the unexpected happened—an accident. There was no uprising of the people, but they were restive; and the Democratic party leaders, thinking to gain some independent votes, decided to raise the cry "reform" and put up a ticket of candidates different enough from the usual offerings of political parties to give color to their platform. These leaders were not in earnest. There was little difference between the two parties in the city; but the rascals that were in had been getting the greater share of the spoils, and the "outs" wanted more than was given to them. "Boodle" was not the issue, no exposures were made or threatened, and the bosses expected to control their men if elected. Simply as part of the game, the Democrats raised the slogan, "reform" and "no more Ziegenheinism."

Mayor Ziegenhein, called "Uncle Henry," was a "good fellow," "one of the boys," and though it was during his administration that the city grew ripe and went to rot, his opponents talked only of incompetence and neglect, and repeated such stories as that of his famous reply to some citizens who complained because certain street lights were put out: "You have the moon yet—ain't it?"

When somebody mentioned Joseph W. Folk for Circuit Attorney the leaders were ready to accept him. They didn't know much about him. He was a young man from Tennessee; had been President of the Jefferson Club, and arbitrated the railroad strike of 1898. But Folk did not want the place. He was a civil lawyer, had had no practice at the criminal bar, cared little about it, and a lucrative business as counsel for corporations was interesting him. He rejected the invitation. The committee called again and again, urging his duty to his party, and the city, etc.

"Very well," he said, at last, "I will accept the nomination, but if elected I will do my duty. There must be no attempt to influence my actions when I am called upon to punish lawbreakers."

The committeemen took such statements as the conventional platitudes of candidates. They nominated him, the Democratic ticket was elected, and Folk became Circuit Attorney for the Eighth Missouri District.

Three weeks after taking the oath of office his campaign pledges were put to the test. A number of arrests had been made in connection with the recent election, and charges of illegal registration were preferred against men of both parties. Mr. Folk took them up like routine cases of ordinary crime. Political bosses rushed to the rescue. Mr. Folk was reminded of his duty to his party, and told that he was expected to construe the law in such a manner that repeaters and other election criminals who had hoisted Democracy's flag and helped elect him might be either discharged or receive the minimum punishment. The nature of the young lawyer's reply can best be inferred from the words of that veteran political leader, Colonel Ed Butler, who, after a visit to Mr. Folk, wrathfully exclaimed, "D—n Joe! he thinks he's the whole thing as Circuit Attorney."

The election cases were passed through the courts with astonishing rapidity; no more mercy was shown Democrats than Republicans, and before winter came a number of ward heelers and old-time party workers were behind the bars in Jefferson City. He next turned his attention to grafters and straw bondsmen with whom the courts were infested, and several of these leeches are in the penitentiary to-day. The business was broken up because of his activity. But Mr. Folk had made little more than the beginning.

One afternoon, late in January, 1903, a newspaper reporter, known as "Red" Galvin, called Mr. Folk's attention to a ten-line newspaper item to the effect that a large sum of money had been placed in a bank for the purpose of bribing certain Assemblymen to secure the passage of a street railroad ordinance. No names were mentioned, but Mr. Galvin surmised that the bill referred to was one introduced on behalf of the Suburban Railway Company. An hour later Mr. Folk sent the names of nearly one hundred persons to the sheriff, with instructions to subpœna them before the grand jury at once. The list included Councilmen, members of the House of Delegates, officers and directors of the Suburban Railway, bank presidents and cashiers. In three days the investigation was being pushed with vigor, but St. Louis was laughing at the "huge joke." Such things had been attempted before. The men who had been ordered to appear before the grand jury jested as they chatted in the anterooms, and newspaper accounts of these preliminary examinations were written in the spirit of burlesque.

It has developed since that Circuit Attorney Folk knew nothing, and was not able to learn much more during the first days; but he says he saw here and there puffs of smoke and he determined to find the fire. It was not an easy job. The first break into such a system is always difficult. Mr. Folk began with nothing but courage and a strong personal conviction. He caused peremptory summons to be issued, for the immediate attendance in the grand jury room of Charles H. Turner, president of the Suburban Railway, and Philip Stock, a representative of brewers' interests, who, he had reason to believe, was the legislative agent in this deal.

"Gentlemen," said Mr. Folk, "I have secured sufficient evidence to warrant the return of indictments against you for bribery, and I shall prosecute you to the full extent of the law and send you to the penitentiary unless you tell to this grand jury the complete history of the corruptionist methods employed by you to secure the passage of Ordinance No. 44. I shall give you three days to consider the matter. At the end of that time, if you have not returned here and given us the information demanded, warrants will be issued for your arrest."

They looked at the audacious young prosecutor and left the Four Courts building without uttering a word. He waited. Two days later, ex-Lieutenant Governor Charles P. Johnson, the veteran criminal lawyer, called, and said that his client, Mr. Stock, was in such poor health that he would be unable to appear before the grand jury.

"I am truly sorry that Mr. Stock is ill," replied Mr.

Folk, "for his presence here is imperative, and if he fails to appear he will be arrested before sundown."

That evening a conference was held in Governor Johnson's office, and the next day this story was told in the grand jury room by Charles H. Turner, millionaire president of the Suburban Railway, and corroborated by Philip Stock, man-about-town and a good fellow: The Suburban, anxious to sell out at a large profit to its only competitor, the St. Louis Transit Co., caused to be drafted the measure known as House Bill No. 44. So sweeping were its grants that Mr. Turner, who planned and executed the document, told the directors in his confidence that its enactment into law would enhance the value of the property from three to six million dollars. The bill introduced, Mr. Turner visited Colonel Butler, who had long been known as a legislative agent, and asked his price for securing the passage of the measure. "One hundred and forty-five thousand dollars will be my fee," was the reply. The railway president demurred. He would think the matter over, he said, and he hired a cheaper man, Mr. Stock. Stock conferred with the representative of the combine in the House of Delegates and reported that $75,000 would be necessary in this branch of the Assembly. Mr. Turner presented a note indorsed by two of the directors whom he could trust, and secured a loan from the German American Savings Bank.

Bribe funds in pocket, the legislative agent telephoned John Murrell, at that time a representative of the House combine, to meet him in the office of the Lincoln Trust Company. There the two rented a safe-deposit box. Mr. Stock placed in the drawer the roll of $75,000, and each subscribed to an agreement that the box should not be opened unless both were present. Of course the conditions spread upon the bank's daybook made no reference to the purpose for which this fund had been deposited, but an agreement entered into by Messrs. Stock and Murrell was to the effect that the $75,000 should be given Mr. Murrell as soon as the bill became an ordinance, and by him distributed to the members of the combine. Stock turned to the Council, and upon his report a further sum of $60,000 was secured. These bills were placed in a safe-deposit box of the Mississippi Valley Trust Co., and the man who held the key as representative of the Council combine was Charles H. Kratz.

All seemed well, but a few weeks after placing these funds in escrow, Mr. Stock reported to his employer that there was an unexpected hitch due to the action of Emil Meysenburg, who, as a member of the Council Committee on Railroads, was holding up the report on the bill. Mr. Stock said that Mr. Meysenburg held some worthless shares in a defunct corporation and wanted Mr. Stock to purchase this paper at its par value of $9,000. Mr. Turner gave Mr. Stock the money with which to buy the shares.

Thus the passage of House Bill 44 promised to cost the Suburban Railway Co. $144,000, only one thousand dollars less than that originally named by the political boss to whom Mr. Turner had first applied. The bill, however, passed both houses of the Assembly. The sworn servants of the city had done their work and held out their hands for the bribe money.

Then came a court mandate which prevented the Suburban Railway Co. from reaping the benefit of the vote-buying, and Charles H. Turner, angered at the check, issued orders that the money in safe-deposit boxes should not be touched. War was declared between bribe-givers and bribe-takers, and the latter resorted to tactics which they hoped would frighten the Suburban people into submission—such as making enough of the story public to cause rumors of impending prosecution. It was that first item which Mr. Folk saw and acted upon.

When Messrs. Turner and Stock unfolded in the grand jury room the details of their bribery plot, Circuit Attorney Folk found himself in possession of verbal evidence of a great crime; he needed as material exhibits the two large sums of money in safe-deposit vaults of two of the largest banking institutions of the West. Had this money been withdrawn? Could he get it if it was there? Lock-boxes had always been considered sacred and beyond the power of the law to open. "I've always held," said Mr. Folk, "that the fact that a thing never had been done was no reason for thinking it couldn't be done." He decided in this case that the magnitude of the interests involved warranted unusual action, so he selected a committee of grand jurors and visited one of the banks. He told the president, a personal friend, the facts that had come into his possession, and asked permission to search for the fund.

"Impossible," was the reply. "Our rules deny anyone the right."

"Mr. ——," said Mr. Folk, "a crime has been committed, and you hold concealed the principal evidence thereto. In the name of the State of Missouri I demand that you cause the box to be opened. If you refuse, I shall cause a warrant to be issued, charging you as an accessory."

For a minute not a word was spoken by anyone in the room; then the banker said in almost inaudible tones:

"Give me a little time, gentlemen. I must consult with our legal adviser before taking such a step."

"We will wait ten minutes," said the Circuit Attorney. "By that time we must have access to the vault or a warrant will be applied for."

At the expiration of that time a solemn procession wended its way from the president's office to the vaults in the sub-cellar—the president, the cashier, and the corporation's lawyer, the grand jurors, and the Circuit Attorney. All bent eagerly forward as the key was inserted in the lock. The iron drawer yielded, and a roll of something wrapped in brown paper was brought to light. The Circuit Attorney removed the rubber bands, and national bank notes of large denomination spread out flat before them. The money was counted, and the sum was $75,000!

The boodle fund was returned to its repository, officers of the bank were told they would be held responsible for it until the courts could act. The investigators visited the other financial institution. They met with more resistance there. The threat to procure a warrant had no effect until Mr. Folk left the building and set off in the direction of the Four Courts. Then a messenger called him back, and the second box was opened. In this was found $60,000. The chain of evidence was complete.

From that moment events moved rapidly. Charles Kratz and John K. Murrell, alleged representatives of Council and House combines, were arrested on bench warrants and placed under heavy bonds. Kratz was brought into court from a meeting at which plans were being formed for his election to the National Congress. Murrell was taken from his undertaking establishment. Emil Meysenburg, millionaire broker, was seated in his office when a sheriff's deputy entered and read a document that charged him with bribery. The summons reached Henry Nicolaus while he was seated at his desk, and the wealthy brewer was compelled to send for a bondsman to avoid passing a night in jail. The cable flashed the news to Cairo, Egypt, that Ellis Wainwright, many times a millionaire, proprietor of the St. Louis brewery that bears this name, had been indicted. Julius Lehmann, one of the members of the House of Delegates, who had joked while waiting in the grand jury's anteroom, had his laughter cut short by the hand of a deputy sheriff on his shoulder and the words, "You are charged with perjury." He was joined at the bar of the criminal court by Harry Faulkner, another jolly good fellow.

Consternation spread among the boodle gang. Some of the men took night trains for other States and foreign countries; the majority remained and counseled together. Within twenty-four hours after the first indictments were returned, a meeting of bribe-givers and bribe-takers was held in South St. Louis. The total wealth of those in attendance was $30,000,000, and their combined political influence sufficient to carry any municipal election under normal conditions.

This great power was aligned in opposition to one man, who still was alone. It was not until many indictments had been returned that a citizens' committee was formed to furnish funds, and even then most of the contributors concealed their identity. Mr. James L. Blair, the treasurer, testified in court that they were afraid to be known lest "it ruin their business."

At the meeting of corruptionists three courses were decided upon. Political leaders were to work on the Circuit Attorney by promise of future reward, or by threats. Detectives were to ferret out of the young lawyer's past anything that could be used against him. Witnesses would be sent out of town and provided with money to remain away until the adjournment of the grand jury.

Mr. Folk at once felt the pressure, and it was of a character to startle one. Statesmen, lawyers, merchants, clubmen, churchmen—in fact, men prominent in all walks of life—visited him at his office and at his home, and urged that he cease such activity against his fellow-townspeople. Political preferment was promised if he would yield; a political grave if he persisted. Threatening letters came, warning him of plots to murder, to disfigure, and to blackguard. Word came from Tennessee that detectives were investigating every act of his life. Mr. Folk told the politicians that he was not seeking political favors, and not looking forward to another office; the others he defied. Meantime he probed the deeper into the municipal sore. With his first successes for prestige and aided by the panic among the boodlers, he soon had them suspicious of one another, exchanging charges of betrayal, and ready to "squeal" or run at the slightest sign of danger. One member of the House of Delegates became so frightened while under the inquisitorial cross-fire that he was seized with a nervous chill; his false teeth fell to the floor, and the rattle so increased his alarm that he rushed from the room without stopping to pick up his teeth, and boarded the next train.

It was not long before Mr. Folk had dug up the intimate history of ten years of corruption, especially of the business of the North and South and the Central Traction franchise grants, the last-named being even more iniquitous than the Suburban.

Early in 1898 a "promoter" rented a bridal suite at the Planters' Hotel, and having stocked the rooms with wines, liquors, and cigars until they resembled a candidate's headquarters during a convention, sought introduction to members of the Assembly and to such political bosses as had influence with the city fathers. Two weeks after his arrival the Central Traction bill was introduced "by request" in the Council. The measure was a blanket franchise, granting rights of way which had not been given to old-established companies, and permitting the beneficiaries to parallel any track in the city. It passed both Houses despite the protests of every newspaper in the city, save one, and was vetoed by the mayor. The cost to the promoter was $145,000.

Preparations were made to pass the bill over the executive's veto. The bridal suite was restocked, larger sums of money were placed on deposit in the banks, and the services of three legislative agents were engaged. Evidence now in the possession of the St. Louis courts tells in detail the disposition of $250,000 of bribe money. Sworn statements prove that $75,000 was spent in the House of Delegates. The remainder of the $250,000 was distributed in the Council, whose members, though few in number, appraised their honor at a higher figure on account of their higher positions in the business and social world. Finally, but one vote was needed to complete the necessary two-thirds in the upper Chamber. To secure this a councilman of reputed integrity was paid $50,000 in consideration that he vote aye when the ordinance should come up for final passage. But the promoter did not dare risk all upon the vote of one man, and he made this novel proposition to another honored member, who accepted it:

"You will vote on roll call after Mr. ——. I will place $45,000 in the hands of your son, which amount will become yours, if you have to vote for the measure because of Mr. ——'s not keeping his promise. But if he stands out for it you can vote against it, and the money shall revert to me."

On the evening when the bill was read for final passage the City Hall was crowded with ward heelers and lesser politicians. These men had been engaged by the promoter, at five and ten dollars a head, to cheer on the boodling Assemblymen. The bill passed the House with a rush, and all crowded into the Council Chamber. While the roll was being called the silence was profound, for all knew that some men in the Chamber whose reputations had been free from blemish, were under promise and pay to part with honor that night. When the clerk was two-thirds down the list those who had kept count knew that but one vote was needed. One more name was called. The man addressed turned red, then white, and after a moment's hesitation he whispered "Aye"! The silence was so death-like that his vote was heard throughout the room, and those near enough heard also the sigh of relief that escaped from the member who could now vote "no" and save his reputation.

The Central Franchise bill was a law, passed over the mayor's veto. The promoter had expended nearly $300,000 in securing the legislation, but within a week he sold his rights of way to "Eastern capitalists" for $1,250,000. The United Railways Company was formed, and without owning an inch of steel rail, or a plank in a car, was able to compel every street railroad in St. Louis, with the exception of the Suburban, to part with stock and right of way and agree to a merger. Out of this grew the St. Louis Transit Company of to-day.

Several incidents followed this legislative session. After the Assembly had adjourned, a promoter entertained the

$50,000 councilman at a downtown restaurant. During the supper the host remarked to his guest, "I wish you would lend me that $50,000 until to-morrow. There are some of the boys outside whom I haven't paid." The money changed hands. The next day, having waited in vain for the promoter, Mr. Councilman armed himself with a revolver and began a search of the hotels. The hunt in St. Louis proved fruitless, but the irate legislator kept on the trail until he came face to face with the lobbyist in the corridor of the Waldorf-Astoria. The New Yorker, seeing the danger, seized the St. Louisan by the arm and said soothingly, "There, there; don't take on so. I was called away suddenly. Come to supper with me; I will give you the money."

The invitation was accepted, and champagne soon was flowing. When the man from the West had become sufficiently maudlin the promoter passed over to him a letter, which he had dictated to a typewriter while away from the table for a few minutes. The statement denied all knowledge of bribery.

"You sign that and I will pay you $5,000. Refuse, and you don't get a cent," said the promoter. The St. Louisan returned home carrying the $5,000, and that was all.

Meanwhile the promoter had not fared so well with other spoilsmen. By the terms of the ante-legislation agreement referred to above, the son of one councilman was pledged to return $45,000 if his father was saved the necessity of voting for the bill. The next day the New Yorker sought out this young man and asked for the money.

"I am not going to give it to you," was the cool rejoinder. "My mamma says that it is bribe money and that it would be wrong to give it to either you or father, so I shall keep it myself." And he did. When summoned before the grand jury this young man asked to be relieved from answering questions. "I am afraid I might commit perjury," he said. He was advised to "Tell the truth and there will be no risk."

"It would be all right," said the son, "if Mr. Folk would tell me what the other fellows have testified to. Please have him do that."

Two indictments were found as the result of this Central Traction bill, and bench warrants were served on Robert M. Snyder and George J. Kobusch. The State charged the former with being one of the promoters of the bill, the definite allegation being bribery. Mr. Kobusch, who is president of a street car manufacturing company, was charged with perjury.

The first case tried was that of Emil Meysenburg, the millionaire who compelled the Suburban people to purchase his worthless stock. He was defended by three attorneys of high repute in criminal jurisprudence, but the young Circuit Attorney proved equal to the emergency, and a conviction was secured. Three years in the penitentiary was the sentence. Charles Kratz, the Congressional candidate, forfeited $40,000 by flight, and John K. Murrell also disappeared. Mr. Folk traced Murrell to Mexico, caused his arrest in Guadalajara, negotiated with the authorities for his surrender, and when this failed, arranged for his return home to confess, and his evidence brought about the indictment, on September 8, of eighteen members of the municipal legislature. The second case was that of Julius Lehmann. Two years at hard labor was the sentence, and the man who had led the jokers in the grand jury anteroom would have fallen when he heard it, had not a friend been standing near.

Besides the convictions of these and other men of good standing in the community, and the flight of many more, partnerships were dissolved, companies had to be reorganized, business houses were closed because their proprietors were absent, but Mr. Folk, deterred as little by success as by failure, moved right on; he was not elated; he was not sorrowful. The man proceeded with his work quickly, surely, smilingly, without fear or pity. The terror spread, and the rout was complete.

When another grand jury was sworn and proceeded to take testimony there were scores of men who threw up their hands and crying *"Mea culpa!"* begged to be permitted to tell all they knew and not be prosecuted. The inquiry broadened. The son of a former mayor was indicted for misconduct in office while serving as his father's private secretary, and the grand jury recommended that the ex-mayor be sued in the civil courts, to recover interests on public money which he had placed in his own pocket. A true bill fell on a former City Register, and more Assemblymen were arrested, charged with making illegal contracts with the city. At last the ax struck upon the trunk of the greatest oak of the forest. Colonel Butler, the boss who has controlled elections in St. Louis for many years, the millionaire who had risen from bellows-boy in a blacksmith's shop to be the maker and guide of the Governors of Missouri, one of the men who helped nominate and elect Folk—he also was indicted on two counts charging attempted bribery. That Butler has controlled legislation in St. Louis had long been known. It was generally understood that he owned Assemblymen before they ever took the oath of office, and that he did not have to pay for votes. And yet open bribery was the allegation now. Two members of the Board of Health stood ready to swear that he offered them $2,500 for their approval of a garbage contract.

Pitiful? Yes, but typical. Other cities are today in the same condition as St. Louis before Mr. Folk was invited in to see its rottenness. Chicago is cleaning itself up just now, so is Minneapolis, and Pittsburg recently had a bribery scandal; Boston is at peace, Cincinnati and St. Paul are satisfied, while Philadelphia is happy with the worst government in the world. As for the small towns and the villages, many of these are busy as bees at the loot.

St. Louis, indeed, in its disgrace, has a great advantage. It was exposed late; it has not been reformed and caught again and again, until its citizens are reconciled to corruption. But, best of all, the man who has turned St. Louis inside out, turned it, as it were, upside down, too. In all cities, the better classes—the business men—are the sources of corruption; but they are so rarely pursued and caught that we do not fully realize whence the trouble comes. Thus most cities blame the politicians and the ignorant and vicious poor.

Mr. Folk has shown St. Louis that its bankers, brokers, corporation officers,—its business men are the sources of evil, so that from the start it will know the municipal problem in its true light. With a tradition for public spirit, it may drop Butler and its runaway bankers, brokers, and brewers, and pushing aside the scruples of the hundreds of men down in blue book, and red book, and church register, who are lying hidden behind the statutes of limitations, the city may restore good government. Otherwise the exposures by Mr. Folk will result only in the perfection of the corrupt system. For the corrupt can learn a lesson when the good citizens cannot. The Tweed régime in New York taught Tammany to organize its boodle business; the police exposure taught it to improve its method of collecting blackmail. And both now are almost perfect and safe. The rascals of St. Louis will learn in like manner; they will concentrate the control of their bribery system, excluding from the profit-sharing the great mass of weak rascals, and carrying on the business as a business in the interest of a trustworthy few. District Attorney Jerome cannot catch the Tammany men, and Circuit Attorney Folk will not be able another time to break the St. Louis ring. This is St. Louis' one great chance.

But, for the rest of us, it does not matter about St. Louis any more than it matters about Colonel Butler *et al.* The point is, that what went on in St. Louis is going on in most of our cities, towns, and villages. The problem of municipal government in America has not been solved. The people may be tired of it, but they cannot give it up —not yet.

The Shame of Minneapolis

(*January, 1903*)

Whenever anything extraordinary is done in American municipal politics, whether for good or for evil, you can trace it almost invariably to one man. The people do not do it. Neither do the "gangs," "combines," or political parties. These are but instruments by which bosses (not leaders; we Americans are not led, but driven) rule the people, and commonly sell them out. But there are at least two forms of the autocracy which has supplanted the democracy here as it has everywhere democracy has been tried. One is that of the organized majority by which, as with the Republican machine in Philadelphia, the boss has normal control of more than half the voters. The other is that of the adroitly managed minority. The "good people" are herded into parties and stupefied with convictions and a name, Republican or Democrat; while the "bad people" are so organized or interested by the boss that he can wield their votes to enforce terms with party managers and decide elections. St. Louis is a conspicuous example of this form. Minneapolis is another. Colonel Ed Butler is the unscrupulous opportunist who handled the non-partisan minority which turned St. Louis into a "boodle town." In Minneapolis "Doc" Ames was the man.

Minneapolis is a New England town on the upper Mississippi. The metropolis of the Northwest, it is the metropolis also of Norway and Sweden in America. Indeed, it is the second largest Scandinavian city in the world. But Yankees, straight from Down East, settled the town, and their New England spirit predominates. They had Bayard Taylor lecture there in the early days of the settlement; they made it the seat of the University of Minnesota. Yet even now, when the town has grown to a population of more than 200,000, you feel that there is something Western about it too—a Yankee with a round Puritan head, an open prairie heart, and a great, big Scandinavian body. The "Roundhead" takes the "Squarehead" out into the woods, and they cut lumber by forests, or they go out on the prairies and raise wheat and mill it into fleet-cargoes of flour. They work hard, they make money, they are sober, satisfied, busy with their own affairs. There isn't much time for public business. Taken together, Miles, Hans, and Ole are very American. Miles insists upon strict laws, Ole and Hans want one or two Scandinavians on their ticket. These things granted, they go off on raft or reaper, leaving whoso will to enforce the laws and run the city.

The people who were left to govern the city hated above all things strict laws. They were the loafers, saloon keepers, gamblers, criminals, and the thriftless poor of all nationalities. Resenting the sobriety of a staid, industrious community, and having no Irish to boss them, they delighted to follow the jovial pioneer doctor, Albert Alonzo Ames. He was the "good fellow"—a genial, generous reprobate. Devery, Tweed, and many more have exposed in vain this amiable type. "Doc" Ames, tall, straight, and cheerful, attracted men, and they gave him votes for his smiles. He stood for license. There was nothing of the Puritan about him. His father, the sturdy old pioneer, Dr. Alfred Elisha Ames, had a strong strain of it in him, but he moved on with his family of six sons from Garden Prairie, Ill., to Fort Snelling reservation, in 1851, before Minneapolis was founded, and young Albert Alonzo, who then was ten years old, grew up free, easy, and tolerant. He was sent to school, then to college in Chicago, and he returned home a doctor of medicine before he was twenty-one. As the town waxed soberer and richer, "Doc" grew gayer and more and more generous. Skillful as a surgeon, devoted as a physician, and as a man kindly, he increased his practice till he was the best-loved man in the community. He was especially good to the poor. Anybody could summon "Doc" Ames at any hour to any distance. He went, and he gave not only his professional service, but sympathy, and often charity. "Richer men than you will pay your bill," he told the destitute. So there was a basis for his "good-fellowship." There always is; these good fellows are not frauds—not in the beginning.

But there is another side to them sometimes. Ames was sunshine not to the sick and destitute only. To the vicious and the depraved also he was a comfort. If a man was a hard drinker, the good Doctor cheered him with another drink; if he had stolen something, the Doctor helped to get him off. He was naturally vain; popularity developed his love of approbation. His loose life brought disapproval only from the good people, so gradually the Doctor came to enjoy best the society of the barroom and the streets. This society, flattered in turn, worshiped the good Doctor, and, active in politics always, put its physician into the arena.

Had he been wise or even shrewd, he might have made himself a real power. But he wasn't calculating, only light and frivolous, so he did not organize his forces and run men for office. He sought office himself from the start, and he got most of the small places he wanted by changing his party to seize the opportunity. His floating minority, added to the regular partisan vote, was sufficient ordinarily for his useless victories. As time went on he rose from smaller offices to be a Republican mayor, then twice at intervals to be a Democratic mayor. He was a candidate once for Congress; he stood for governor once on a sort of Populist-Democrat ticket. Ames could not get anything outside of his own town, however, and after his third term as mayor it was thought he was out of politics altogether. He was getting old, and he was getting worse.

Like many a "good fellow" with hosts of miscellaneous friends downtown to whom he was devoted, the good Doctor neglected his own family. From neglect he went on openly to separation from his wife and a second establishment. The climax came not long before the election of 1900. His wife died. The family would not have the father at the funeral, but he appeared,—not at the house, but in a carriage on the street. He sat across the way, with his feet up and a cigar in his mouth, till the funeral moved; then he circled around, crossing it and meeting it, and making altogether a scene which might well close any man's career.

It didn't end his. The people had just secured the passage of a new primary law to establish direct popular government. There were to be no more nominations by convention. The voters were to ballot for their party candidates. By a slip of some sort, the laws did not specify that Republicans only should vote for Republican candidates, and only Democrats for Democratic candidates. Any voter could vote at either primary. Ames, in disrepute with his own party, the Democratic, bade his followers vote for his nomination for mayor on the Republican ticket. They all voted; not all the Republicans did. He was nominated. Nomination is far from election, and you would say that the trick would not help him. But that was a Presidential year, so the people of Minneapolis had to vote for Ames, the Republican candidate for mayor. Besides, Ames said he was going to reform; that he was getting old, and wanted to close his career with a good administration. The effective argument, however, was that, since McKinley had to be elected to save the country, Ames must be supported for mayor of Minneapolis. Why? The great American people cannot be trusted to scratch a ticket.

Well, Minneapolis got its old mayor back, and he was indeed "reformed." Up to this time Ames had not been very venal personally. He was a "spender," not a "grafter," and he was guilty of corruption chiefly by proxy; he took the honors and left the spoils to his followers. His administrations were no worse than the worst. Now, however, he set out upon a career of corruption which for deliberateness, invention, and avarice has never been equaled. It was as if he had made up his mind that he had been careless long enough, and meant to enrich his last years. He began promptly.

Immediately upon his election, before he took office (on January 7, 1901), he organized a cabinet and laid plans to turn the city over to outlaws who were to work under police direction for the profit of his administration. He chose for chief his brother, Colonel Fred W. Ames, who had recently returned under a cloud from service in the Philippines. But he was a weak vessel for chief of police, and the mayor picked for chief of detectives an abler man, who was to direct the more difficult operations. This was Norman W. King, a former gambler, who knew the criminals needed in the business ahead. King was to invite to Minneapolis thieves, confidence men, pickpockets and gamblers, and release some that were in the local jail. They were to be organized into groups, according to their profession, and detectives were assigned to assist and direct them. The head of the gambling syndicate was to have charge of the gambling, making the terms and collecting the "graft," just as King and a Captain Hill were to collect from the thieves. The collector for women of the town was to be Irwin A. Gardner, a medical student in the Doctor's office, who was made a special policeman for the purpose. These men looked over the force, selected those men who could be trusted, charged them a price for their retention, and marked for dismissal 107 men out of 225, the 107 being the best policemen in the department from the point of view of the citizens who afterward reorganized the force. John Fitchette, better known as "Coffee John," a Virginian (who served on the Jefferson Davis jury), the keeper of a notorious coffee-house, was to be a captain of police, with no duties except to sell places on the police force.

And they did these things that they planned—all and more. The administration opened with the revolution on the police force. The thieves in the local jail were liberated, and it was made known to the Under World generally that "things were doing" in Minneapolis. The incoming swindlers reported to King or his staff for instructions, and went to work, turning the "swag" over to the detectives in charge. Gambling went on openly, and disorderly houses multiplied under the fostering care of Gardner, the medical student. But all this was not enough. Ames dared to break openly into the municipal system of vice protection.

There was such a thing. Minneapolis, strict in its laws, forbade vices which are inevitable, then regularly permitted them under certain conditions. Legal limits, called "patrol lines," were prescribed, within which saloons might be opened. These ran along the river front, out through part of the business section, with long arms reaching into the Scandinavian quarters, north and south. Gambling also was confined, but more narrowly. And there were limits, also arbitrary, but not always identical with those for gambling, within which the social evil was allowed. But the novel feature of this scheme was that disorderly houses were practically licensed by the city, the women appearing before the clerk of the Municipal Court each month to pay a "fine" of $100. Unable at first to get this "graft," Ames's man Gardner persuaded women to start houses, apartments, and, of all things, candy stores, which sold sweets to children and tobacco to the "lumber Jacks" in front, while a nefarious traffic was carried on in the rear. But they paid Ames, not the city, and that was all this "reform" administration cared about.

The revenue from all these sources must have been large. It only whetted the avarice of the mayor and his Cabinet. They let gambling privileges without restriction as to location or "squareness"; the syndicate could cheat and rob as it would. Peddlers and pawnbrokers, formerly licensed by the city, bought permits now instead from the mayor's agent in this field. Some two hundred slot machines were installed in various parts of the town, with owner's agent and mayor's agent watching and collecting from them enough to pay the mayor $15,000 a year as his share. Auction frauds were instituted. Opium joints and unlicensed saloons, called "blind pigs," were protected. Gardner even had a police baseball team, for whose games tickets were sold to people who had to buy them. But the women were the easiest "graft." They were compelled to buy illustrated biographies of the city officials; they had to give presents of money, jewelry, and gold stars to police officers. But the money they still paid direct to the city in fines, some $35,000 a year, fretted the mayor, and at last he reached for it. He came out with a declaration, in his old character as friend of the oppressed, that $100 a month was too much for these women to pay. They should be required to pay the city fine only once in two months. This puzzled the town till it became generally known that Gardner collected the other month for the mayor. The final outrage in this department, however, was an order of the mayor for the periodic visits to disorderly houses, by the city's physicians, at from $5 to $20 per visit. The two physicians he appointed called when they willed, and more and more frequently, till toward the end the calls became a pure

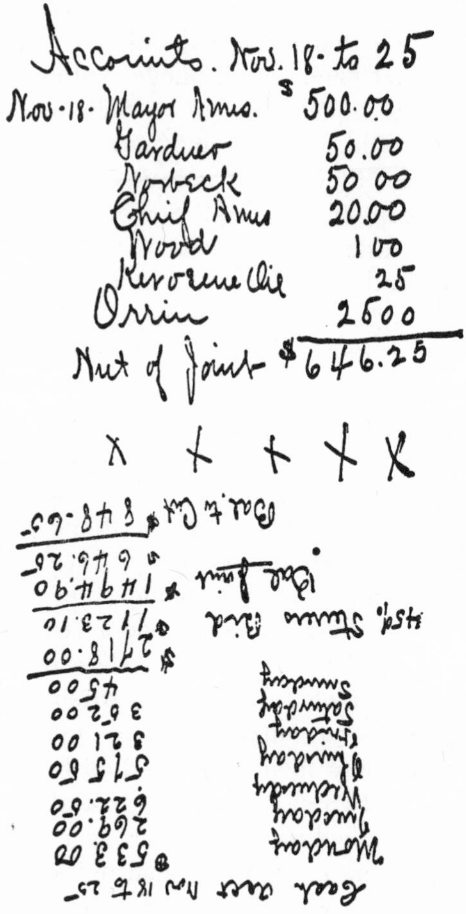

Accounts. Nov. 18 · to 25

Nov · 18 ·	Mayor Amo.	$500.00
	Gardner	50.00
	Norbeck	50 00
	Chief Amo	20.00
	Wood	1 00
	Kerosene Oil	25
	Orrin	2500
	Nut of Joint	$646.25

X X X X X

Facsimile of the first page of "The Big Mitt Ledger"

formality, with the collections as the one and only object.

In a general way all this business was known. It did not arouse the citizens, but it did attract criminals, and more and more thieves and swindlers came hurrying to Minneapolis. Some of them saw the police, and made terms. Some were seen by the police and invited to go to work. There was room for all. This astonishing fact that the government of a city asked criminals to rob the people is fully established. The police and the criminals confessed it separately. Their statements agree in detail. Detective Norbeck made the arrangements, and introduced the swindlers to Gardner, who, over King's head, took the money from them. Here is the story "Billy" Edwards, a "big mitt" man, told under oath of his reception in Minneapolis:

"I had been out to the Coast, and hadn't seen Norbeck for some time. After I returned I boarded a Minneapolis car one evening to go down to South Minneapolis to visit a friend. Norbeck and Detective DeLaittre were on the car. When Norbeck saw me he came up and shook hands, and said, 'Hullo, Billy, how goes it?' I said, 'Not very well.' Then he says, 'Things have changed since you went away. Me and Gardner are the whole thing now. Before you left they thought I didn't know anything, but I turned a few tricks, and now I'm It.' 'I'm glad of that, Chris,' I said. He says, 'I've got great things for you. I'm going to fix up a joint for you.' 'That's good,' I said, 'but I don't believe you can do it.' 'Oh, yes, I can,' he replied. 'I'm It now—Gardner and me.' 'Well, if you can do it,' says I, 'there's money in it.' 'How much can you pay?' he asked. 'Oh, $150 or $200 a week,' says I. 'That settles it,' he said; 'I'll take you down to see Gardner, and we'll fix it up.' Then he made an appointment to meet me the next night, and we went down to Gardner's house together."

There Gardner talked business in general, showed his drawer full of bills, and jokingly asked how Edwards would like to have them. Edwards says:

"I said, 'That looks pretty good to me,' and Gardner told us that he had 'collected' the money from the women he had on his staff, and that he was going to pay it over to the 'old man' when he got back from his hunting trip next morning. Afterward he told me that the mayor had been much pleased with our $500, and that he said everything was all right, and for us to go ahead."

"Link" Crossman, another confidence man who was with Edwards, said that Gardner demanded $1,000 at first, but compromised on $500 for the mayor, $50 for Gardner, and $50 for Norbeck. To the chief, Fred Ames, they gave tips now and then of $25 or $50. "The first week we ran," said Crossman, "I gave Fred $15. Norbeck took me down there. We shook hands, and I handed him an envelope with $15. He pulled out a list of steerers we had sent him, and said he wanted to go over them with me. He asked where the joint was located. At another time I slipped $25 into his hand as he was standing in the hallway of City Hall." But these smaller payments, after the first "opening, $500," are all down on the pages of the "big mitt" ledger, photographs of which illuminate this article. This notorious book, which was kept by Charlie Howard, one of the "big mitt" men, was much talked of at the subsequent trials, but was kept hidden to await the trial of the mayor himself.

The "big mitt" game was swindling by means of a stacked hand at stud poker. "Steerers" and "boosters" met "suckers" on the street, at hotels, and railway stations, won their confidence, and led them to the "joint." Usually

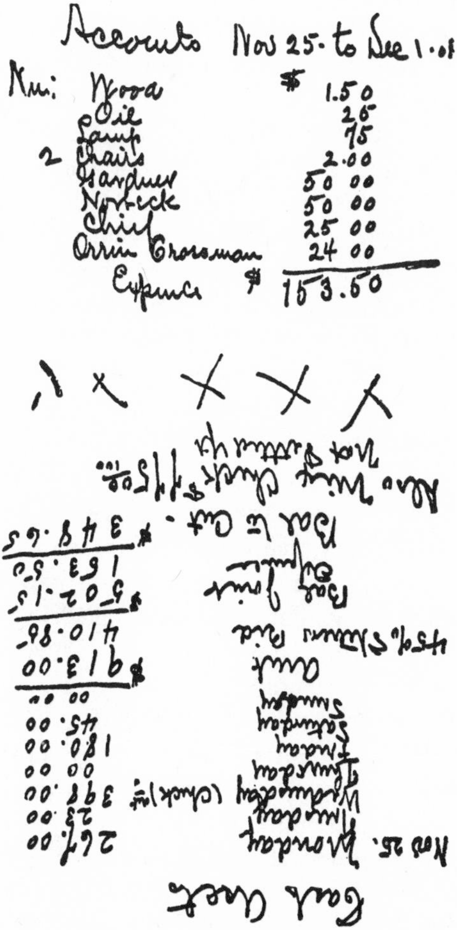

Accounts Nov 25- to Dec 1.08
Nu: Wood $ 1.50
Oil 25
Lamp 75
2 Chairs 2.00
Gardner 50 00
Norbeck 50 00
Chief 25 00
Orrin Crossman 24 00
Expence $ 153.50

Page from "The Big Mitt Ledger": This shows an item concerning the check for $775, which the "sucker" Meix (here spelled Mix) wished not to have honored.

the "sucker" was called, by the amount of his loss, "the $102-man" or "the $35-man." Roman Meix alone had the distinction among all the Minneapolis victims of going by his own name. Having lost $775, he became known for his persistent complainings. But they all "kicked" some. To Detective Norbeck at the street door was assigned the duty of hearing their complaints, and "throwing a scare into them." "Oh, so you've been gambling," he would say. "Have you got a license? Well, then, you better get right out of this town." Sometimes he accompanied them to the station and saw them off. If they were not to be put off thus, he directed them to the chief of police. Fred Ames tried to wear them out by keeping them waiting in the anteroom. If they outlasted him, he saw them and frightened them with threats of all sorts of trouble for gambling without a license. Meix wanted to have payment on his check stopped. Ames, who had been a bank clerk, told him of his banking experience, and then had the effrontery to say that payment on such a check could not be stopped.

Burglaries were common. How many the police planned may never be known. Charles F. Brackett and Fred Malone, police captains and detectives, were active, and one well-established crime of theirs is the robbery of the Pabst Brewing Company office. They persuaded two men, one an employee, to learn the combination of the safe, open and clean it out one night, while the two officers stood guard outside.

The excesses of the municipal administration became so notorious that some of the members of it remonstrated with the others, and certain county officers were genuinely alarmed. No restraint followed their warnings. Sheriff Megaarden, no Puritan himself, felt constrained to

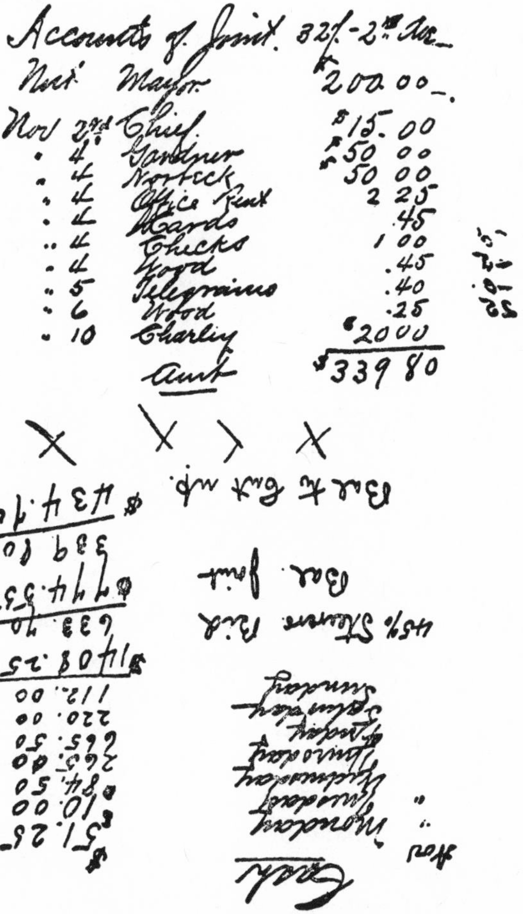

Accounts of Joint. 32½ - 2nd Ave.

Nov	Mayor	$200 00
Nov 2nd	Chief	$15 00
" 4	Gardner	$50 00
" 4	Norbeck	50 00
" 4	Office Rent	2 25
" 4	Cards	.45
" 4	Checks	1 00
" 4	Food	.45
" 5	Telegrams	.40
" 6	Wood	.25
" 10	Charley	$20 00
	Amt	$339 80

Page from "The Big Mitt Ledger": This shows the accounts for a week of small transactions.

interfere, and he made some arrests of gamblers. The Ames people turned upon him in a fury; they accused him of making overcharges in his accounts with the county for fees, and, laying the evidence before Governor Van Sant, they had Megaarden removed from office. Ames offered bribes to two county commissioners to appoint Gardner sheriff, so as to be sure of no more trouble in that quarter. This move failed, but the lesson taught Megaarden served to clear the atmosphere, and the spoliation went on as recklessly as ever. It became impossible.

Even lawlessness must be regulated. Dr. Ames, never an organizer, attempted no control, and his followers began to quarrel among themselves. They deceived one another; they robbed the thieves; they robbed Ames himself. His brother became dissatisfied with his share of the spoils, and formed cabals with captains who plotted against the administration and set up disorderly houses, "panel games," and all sorts of "grafts" of their own.

The one man loyal to the mayor was Gardner; and Fred Ames, Captain King, and their pals plotted the fall of the favorite. Now anybody could get anything from the Doctor, if he could have him alone. The Fred Ames clique chose a time when the mayor was at West Baden; they filled him with suspicion of Gardner and the fear of exposure, and induced him to let a creature named "Reddy" Cohen, instead of Gardner, do the collecting, and pay over all the moneys, not directly, but through Fred. Gardner made a touching appeal. "I have been honest. I have paid you all," he said to the mayor. "Fred and the rest will rob you." This was true, but it was of no avail.

Fred Ames was in charge at last, and he himself went about giving notice of the change. Three detectives were with him when he visited the women, and here is the women's story, in the words of one, as it was told again and again in court: "Colonel Ames came in with the detectives. He stepped into a side room and asked me if I had been paying Gardner. I told him I had, and he told me not to pay no more, but to come to his office later, and he would let me know what to do. I went to the City Hall in about three weeks, after Cohen had called and said he was 'the party.' I asked the chief if it was all right to pay Cohen, and he said it was."

The new arrangement did not work so smoothly as the old. Cohen was an oppressive collector, and Fred Ames, appealed to, was weak and lenient. He had no sure hold on the force. His captains, free of Gardner, were undermining the chief. They increased their private operations. Some of the detectives began to drink hard and neglect their work. Norbeck so worried the "big mitt" men by staying away from the joint, that they complained to Fred about him. The chief rebuked Norbeck, and he promised to "do better," but thereafter he was paid, not by the week, but by piece work—so much for each "trimmed sucker" that he ran out of town. Protected swindlers were arrested for operating in the street by "Coffee John's" new policemen, who took the places of the negligent detectives. Fred let the indignant prisoners go when they were brought before him, but the arrests were annoying, inconvenient, and disturbed business. The whole system became so demoralized that every man was for himself. There was not left even the traditional honor among thieves.

It was at this juncture, in April, 1902, that the grand jury for the summer term was drawn. An ordinary body of unselected citizens, it received no special instructions from the bench; the county prosecutor offered it only routine work to do. But there was a man among them who was a fighter—the foreman, Hovey C. Clarke. He was of an old New England family. Coming to Minneapolis when a young man, seventeen years before, he had fought for employment, fought with his employers for position, fought with his employees, the lumber Jacks, for command, fought for his company against competitors; and he had won always, till now he had the habit of command, the impatient, imperious manner of the master, and the assurance of success which begets it. He did not want to be a grand juryman, he did not want to be a foreman; but since he was both, he wanted to accomplish something.

Why not rip up the Ames gang? Heads shook, hands went up; it was useless to try. The discouragement fired Clarke. That was just what he would do, he said, and he took stock of his jury. Two or three were men with backbone; that he knew, and he quickly had them with him. The rest were all sorts of men. Mr. Clarke won over each man to himself, and interested them all. Then he called for the county prosecutor. The prosecutor was a politician; he knew the Ames crowd; they were too powerful to attack.

"You are excused," said the foreman.

There was a scene; the prosecutor knew his rights.

"Do you think, Mr. Clarke," he cried, "that you can run the grand jury and my office, too?"

"Yes," said Clarke, "I will run your office if I want to; and I want to. You're excused."

Mr. Clarke does not talk much about his doings that summer; he isn't the talking sort. But he does say that all he did was to apply simple business methods to his problem. In action, however, these turned out to be the most approved police methods. He hired a lot of local detectives who, he knew, would talk about what they were doing, and thus would be watched by the police. Having thus thrown a false scent, he hired some other detectives whom nobody knew about. This was expensive; so were many of the other things he did; but he was bound to win, so he paid the price, drawing freely on his own and his colleagues' pockets. (The total cost to the county for a long summer's work by this grand jury was $259.) With his detectives out, he himself went to the jail to get tips from the inside, from criminals who, being there, must have grievances. He made the acquaintance of the jailer, Captain Alexander, and Alexander was a friend of Sheriff Megaarden. Yes, he had some men there who were "sore" and might want to get even.

Now two of these were "big mitt" men who had worked for Gardner. One was "Billy" Edwards, the other "Cheerful Charlie" Howard. I heard too many explanations of their plight to choose any one; this general account will cover the ground: In the Ames mêlée, either by mistake, neglect, or for spite growing out of the network of conflicting interests and gangs, they were arrested and arraigned, not before Fred Ames, but before a judge, and held in bail too high for them to furnish. They had paid for an unexpired period of protection, yet could get neither protection nor bail. They were forgotten. "We got the double cross all right," they said, and they bled with their grievance; but squeal, no, sir!—that was "another deal."

But Mr. Clarke had their story, and he was bound to force them to tell it under oath on the stand. If they did, Gardner and Norbeck would be indicted, tried, and probably convicted. In themselves, these men were of no great importance; but they were the key to the situation, and a way up to the mayor. It was worth trying. Mr. Clarke went into the jail with Messrs. Lester Elwood and Willard J. Hield, grand jurors on whom he relied most for delicate work. They stood by while the foreman talked. And the foreman's way of talking was to smile, swear, threaten, and cajole. "Billy" Edwards told me afterwards that he and Howard were finally persuaded to turn State's evidence, because they believed that Mr. Clarke was the kind of a man to keep his promises and fulfill his threats. "We," he said, meaning criminals generally, "are always stacking up against juries and lawyers who want us to holler. We don't, because we see they ain't wise, and won't get there. They're quitters; they can be pulled off. Clarke has a hard eye. I know men. It's my business to size 'em up, and I took him for a winner, and I played in with him against that whole big bunch of easy things that was running things on the bum." The grand jury was ready at the end of three weeks of hard work to find bills. A prosecutor was needed. The public prosecutor was being ignored, but his first assistant and friend, Al J. Smith, was taken in hand by Mr. Clarke. Smith hesitated; he knew better even than the foreman the power and resources of the Ames gang. But he came to believe in Mr. Clarke, just as Edwards had; he was sure the foreman would win; so he went over to his side, and, having once decided, he led the open fighting, and, alone in court, won cases against men who had the best lawyers in the State to defend them. His court record is extraordinary. Moreover, he took over the negotiations with criminals for evidence, Messrs. Clarke, Hield, Elwood, and the other jurors providing means and moral support. These were needed. Bribes were offered to Smith; he was threatened; he was called a fool. But so was Clarke, to whom $28,000 was offered to quit, and for whose slaughter a slugger was hired to come from Chicago. What startled the jury most, however, was the character of the citizens who were sent to them to dissuade them from their course. No reform I ever studied has failed to bring out this phenomenon of virtuous cowardice, the baseness of the decent citizen.

Nothing stopped this jury, however. They had courage. They indicted Gardner, Norbeck, Fred Ames, and many lesser persons. But the gang had courage, too, and raised a defense fund to fight Clarke. Mayor Ames was defiant. Once, when Mr. Clarke called at the City Hall, the mayor met and challenged him. The mayor's heelers were all about him, but Clarke faced him.

"Yes, Doc Ames, I'm after you," he said. "I've been in this town for seventeen years, and all that time you've been a moral leper. I hear you were rotten during the ten years before that. Now I'm going to put you where all contagious things are put—where you cannot contaminate anybody else."

The trial of Gardner came on. Efforts had been made to persuade him to surrender the mayor, but the young man was paid $15,000 "to stand pat," and he went to trial and conviction silent. Other trials followed fast—Norbeck's, Fred Ames's, Chief of Detectives King's. Witnesses who were out of the State were needed, and true testimony from women. There was no county money for extradition, so the grand jurors paid these costs also. They had Meix followed from Michigan down to Mexico and back to Idaho, where they got him, and he was presented in court one day at the trial of Norbeck, who had "steered" him out of town. Norbeck thought Meix was a thousand miles away, and had been bold before. At the sight of him in court he started to his feet, and that night ran away. The jury spent more money in his pursuit, and they caught him. He confessed, but his evidence was not accepted. He was sentenced to three years in State's prison. Men caved all around, but the women were firm, and the first trial of Fred Ames failed. To break the women's faith in the ring, Mayor Ames was indicted for offering the bribe to have Gardner made sheriff—a genuine, but not the best case against him. It brought the women down to the truth, and Fred Ames, retried, was convicted and sentenced to six and a half years in State's prison. King was tried for accessory to felony (helping in the theft of a diamond, which he afterward stole from the thieves), and sentenced to three and a half years in prison. And still the indictments came, with trials following fast. Al Smith resigned with the consent and thanks of the grand jury; his chief, who was to run for the same office again, wanted to try the rest of the cases, and he did very well.

All men were now on the side of law and order. The panic among the "grafters" was laughable, in spite of its hideous significance. Two heads of departments against whom nothing had been shown suddenly ran away, and thus suggested to the grand jury an inquiry which revealed another source of "graft," in the sale of supplies to public institutions and the diversion of great quantities of provisions to the private residences of the mayor and other officials. Mayor Ames, under indictment and heavy bonds for extortion, conspiracy, and bribe-offering, left the State on a night train; a gentleman who knew him by sight saw him sitting up at eleven o'clock in the smoking-room of the sleeping-car, an unlighted cigar in his mouth, his face ashen and drawn, and at six o'clock the next morning he still was sitting there, his cigar still unlighted. He went to West Baden, a health resort in Indiana, a sick and broken man, aging years in a month. The city was without a mayor, the ring was without a leader; cliques ruled, and they pictured one another hanging about the grand-jury room begging leave to turn State's evidence. Tom Brown, the mayor's secretary, was in the mayor's chair; across the hall sat Fred Ames, the chief of police, balancing Brown's light weight. Both were busy forming cliques within the ring. Brown had on his side Coffee John and Police Captain Hill. Ames had Captain "Norm" King (though he had been convicted and had resigned), Captain Krumweide, and Ernest Wheelock, the chief's secretary. Alderman D. Percy Jones, the president of the council, an honorable man, should have taken the chair, but he was in the East; so this unstable equilibrium was all the city had by way of a government.

Then Fred Ames disappeared. The Tom Brown clique had full sway, and took over the police department. This was a shock to everybody, to none more than to the King clique, which joined in the search for Ames. An alderman, Fred M. Powers, who was to run for mayor on the Republican ticket, took charge of the mayor's office, but he was not sure of his authority or clear as to his policy. The grand jury was the real power behind him, and the foreman was telegraphing for Alderman Jones. Meanwhile the cliques were making appeals to Mayor Ames, in West Baden, and each side that saw him received authority to do its will. The Coffee John clique, denied admission to the grand-jury room, turned to Alderman Powers, and were beginning to feel secure, when they heard that Fred Ames was coming back. They rushed around, and obtained an assurance from the exiled mayor that Fred was returning only to resign. Fred—now under conviction—returned, but he did not resign; supported by his friends, he took charge again of the police force. Coffee John besought Alderman Powers to remove the chief, and when the acting mayor proved himself too timid, Coffee John, Tom Brown, and Captain Hill laid a deep plot. They would ask Mayor Ames to remove his brother. This they felt sure they could persuade the "old man" to do. The difficulty was to keep him from changing his mind when the other side should reach his ear. They hit upon a bold expedient. They would urge the "old man" to remove Fred, and then resign himself, so that he could not undo the deed that they wanted done. Coffee John and Captain Hill slipped out of town one night; they reached West Baden on one train and they left for home on the next, with a demand for Fred's resignation in one hand and the mayor's own in the other. Fred Ames did resign, and though the mayor's resignation was laid aside for a while, to avoid the expense of a special election, all looked well for Coffee John and his clique. They had Fred out, and Alderman Powers was to make them great. But Mr. Powers wabbled. No doubt the grand jury spoke to him. At any rate he turned most unexpectedly on both cliques together. He turned out Tom Brown, but he turned out also Coffee John, and he did not make their man chief of police, but another of someone else's selection. A number of resignations was the result, and these the acting mayor accepted, making a clearing of astonished rascals which was very gratifying to the grand jury and to the nervous citizens of Minneapolis.

But the town was not yet easy. The grand jury, which was the actual head of the government, was about to be discharged, and, besides, their work was destructive. A constructive force was now needed, and Alderman Jones was pelted with telegrams from home bidding him hurry back. He did hurry, and when he arrived, the situation was instantly in control. The grand jury prepared to report, for the city had a mind and a will of its own once more. The criminals found it out last.

Percy Jones, as his friends call him, is of the second generation of his family in Minneapolis. His father started him well-to-do, and he went on from where he was started. College graduate and business man, he has a conscience which, however, he has brains enough to question. He is not the fighter, but the slow, sure executive. As an alderman he is the result of a movement begun several years ago by some young men who were convinced by an exposure of a corrupt municipal council that they should go into politics. A few did go in; Jones was one of these few.

The acting mayor was confronted at once with all the hardest problems of municipal government. Vice rose right up to tempt or to fight him. He studied the situation deliberately, and by and by began to settle it point by point, slowly but finally, against all sorts of opposition. One of his first acts was to remove all the proved rascals on the force, putting in their places men who had been removed by Mayor Ames. Another important step was the appointment of a church deacon and personal friend to be chief of police, this on the theory that he wanted at the head of his police a man who could have no sympathy with crime, a man whom he could implicitly trust. Disorderly houses, forbidden by law, were permitted, but only within certain patrol lines, and they were to pay nothing, in either blackmail or "fines." The number and the standing and the point of view of the "good people" who opposed this order was a lesson to Mr. Jones in practical government. One very prominent citizen and church member threatened him for driving women out of two flats owned by him; the rent was the surest means of "support for his wife and children." Mr. Jones enforced his order.

Other interests—saloon-keepers, brewers, etc.—gave him trouble enough, but all these were trifles in comparison with his experience with the gamblers. They represented organized crime, and they asked for a hearing. Mr. Jones gave them some six weeks for negotiations. They proposed a solution. They said that if he would let them (a syndicate) open four gambling places downtown, they would see that no others ran in any part of the city. Mr. Jones pondered and shook his head, drawing them on. They went away, and came back with a better promise. Though they were not the associates of criminals, they knew that class and their plans. No honest police force, unaided, could deal with crime. Thieves would soon be at work again, and what could Mr. Jones do against them with a police force headed by a church deacon? The gamblers offered to control the criminals for the city.

Mr. Jones, deeply interested, declared he did not believe there was any danger of fresh crimes. The gamblers smiled and went away. By an odd coincidence there happened just after that what the papers called "an epidemic of crime." They were petty thefts, but they occupied the mind of the acting mayor. He wondered at their opportuneness. He wondered how the news of them got out.

The gamblers soon reappeared. Hadn't they told Mr. Jones crime would soon be prevalent in town again? They had, indeed, but the mayor was unmoved; "porch climbers" could not frighten him. But this was only the beginning, the gamblers said: the larger crimes would come next. And they went away again. Sure enough, the large crimes came. One, two, three burglaries of jewelry in the houses of well-known people occurred; then there was a fourth, and the fourth was in the house of a relative of the acting mayor. He was seriously amused. The papers had the news promptly, and not from the police.

The gamblers called again. If they could have the exclusive control of gambling in Minneapolis, they would do all that they had promised before, and, if any large burglaries occurred, they would undertake to recover the "swag," and sometimes catch the thief. Mr. Jones was skeptical of their ability to do all this. The gamblers offered to prove it. How? They would get back for Mr. Jones the jewelry recently reported stolen from four houses in town. Mr. Jones expressed a curiosity to see this done, and the gamblers went away. After a few days the stolen jewelry, parcel by parcel, began to return; with all due police-criminal mystery it was delivered to the chief of police.

When the gamblers called again, they found the acting mayor ready to give his decision on their propositions. It was this: There should be no gambling, with police connivance, in the city of Minneapolis during his term of office.

Mr. Jones told me that if he had before him a long term, he certainly would reconsider this answer. He believed he would decide again as he had already, but he would at least give studious reflection to the question —Can a city be governed without any alliance with crime?

It was an open question. He had closed it only for the four months of his emergency administration. Minneapolis should be clean and sweet for a little while at least, and the new administration should begin with a clear deck.

The Shamelessness of St. Louis

(*March, 1903*)

Tweed's classic question, "What are you going to do about it?" is the most humiliating challenge ever delivered by the One Man to the Many. But it was pertinent. It was the question then; it is the question now. Will the people rule? That is what it means. Is democracy possible? The accounts of financial corruption in St. Louis and of police corruption in Minneapolis raised the same question. They were inquiries into American municipal democracy, and, so far as they went, they were pretty complete answers. The people wouldn't rule. They would have flown to arms to resist a czar or a king, but they let a "mucker" oppress and disgrace and sell them out. "Neglect," so they describe their impotence. But when their shame was laid bare, what did they do then? That is what Tweed, the tyrant, wanted to know, and that is what the democracy of this country needs to know.

Minneapolis answered Tweed. With Mayor Ames a fugitive, the city was reformed, and when he was brought back he was tried and convicted. No city ever profited so promptly by the lesson of its shame. The people had nothing to do with the exposure—that was an accident—nor with the reconstruction. Hovey C. Clarke, who attacked the Ames ring, tore it all to pieces; and D. Percy Jones, who re-established the city government, built a well-nigh perfect thing. There was little left for the people to do but choose at the next regular election between two candidates for mayor, one obviously better than the other, but that they did do. They scratched some ten thousand ballots to do their small part decisively and well. So much by way of revolt. The future will bring Minneapolis up to the real test. The men who saved the city this time have organized to keep it safe, and make the memory of "Doc" Ames a civic treasure, and Minneapolis a city without reproach.

Minneapolis may fail, as New York has failed; but at least these two cities could be moved by shame. Not so St. Louis. Joseph W. Folk, the Circuit Attorney, who began alone, is going right on alone, indicting, trying, convicting boodlers, high and low, following the workings of the combine through all of its startling ramifications, and spreading before the people, in the form of testimony given under oath, the confessions by the boodlers themselves of the whole wretched story. St. Louis is unmoved and unashamed. St. Louis seems to me to be something new in the history of the government of the people, by the rascals, for the rich.

"Tweed Days in St. Louis" did not tell half that the St.

Louisans know of the condition of the city. That article described how in 1898, 1899, and 1900, under the administration of Mayor Ziegenhein, boodling developed into the only real business of the city government. Since that article was written, fourteen men have been tried, and half a score have confessed, so that some measure of the magnitude of the business and of the importance of the interests concerned has been given. Then it was related that "combines" of municipal legislators sold rights, privileges, and public franchises for their own individual profit, and at regular schedule rates. Now the free narratives of convicted boodlers have developed the inside history of the combines, with their unfulfilled plans. Then we understood that these combines did the boodling. Now we know that they had a leader, a boss, who, a rich man himself, represented the financial district and prompted the boodling till the system burst. We knew then how Mr. Folk, a man little known, was nominated against his will for Circuit Attorney; how he warned the politicians who named him; how he proceeded against these same men as against ordinary criminals. Now we have these men convicted.

We saw Charles H. Turner, the president of the Suburban Railway Co., and Philip H. Stock, the secretary of the St. Louis Brewing Co., the first to "preach," telling to the grand jury the story of their bribe fund of $144,000, put into safe-deposit vaults, to be paid to the legislators when the Suburban franchise was granted. St. Louis has seen these two men dashing forth "like fire horses," the one (Mr. Turner) from the presidency of the Commonwealth Trust Company, the other from his brewing company secretaryship, to recite again and again in the criminal courts their miserable story, and count over and over for the jury the dirty bills of that bribe fund. And when they had given their testimony, and the boodlers one after another were convicted, these witnesses have hurried back to their places of business and the convicts to their seats in the municipal assembly. This is literally true. In the House of Delegates sit, under sentence, as follows: Charles F. Kelly, two years; Charles J. Denny, three years and five years; Henry A. Faulkner, two years; E. E. Murrell, State's witness, but not tried.* Nay, this House, with such a membership, had the audacity last fall to refuse to pass an appropriation to enable Mr. Folk to go with his investigation and prosecution of boodling.

Right here is the point. In other cities mere exposure has been sufficient to overthrow a corrupt régime. In St. Louis the conviction of the boodlers leaves the felons in control, the system intact, and the people—spectators. It is these people who are interesting—these people, and the system they have made possible.

The convicted boodlers have described the system to me. There was no politics in it—only business. The city of St. Louis is normally Republican. Founded on the home-rule principle, the corporation is a distinct political entity, with no county to confuse it. The State of Missouri, however, is normally Democratic, and the legislature has taken political possession of the city by giving to the Governor the appointment of the Police and Election Boards. With a defective election law, the Democratic boss in the city became its absolute ruler.

This boss is Edward R. Butler, better known as "Colonel Ed," or "Colonel Butler," or just "Boss." He is an Irishman by birth, a master horseshoer by trade, a good fellow—by nature, at first, then by profession. Along in the

* See *Post Scriptum*, end of chapter.

seventies, when he still wore the apron of his trade, and bossed his tough ward, he secured the agency for a certain patent horseshoe which the city railways liked and bought. Useful also as a politician, they gave him a blanket contract to keep all their mules and horses shod. Butler's farrieries glowed all about the town, and his political influence spread with his business; for everywhere big Ed Butler went there went a smile also, and encouragement for your weakness, no matter what it was. Like "Doc" Ames, of Minneapolis—like the "good fellow" everywhere—Butler won men by helping them to wreck themselves. A priest, the Rev. James Coffey, once denounced Butler from the pulpit as a corrupter of youth; at another time a mother knelt in the aisle of a church, and during service audibly called upon Heaven for a visitation of affliction upon Butler for having ruined her son. These and similar incidents increased his power by advertising it. He grew bolder. He has been known to walk out of a voting-place and call across a cordon of police to a group of men at the curb, "Are there any more repeaters out here that want to vote again?"

They will tell you in St. Louis that Butler never did have much real power, that his boldness and the clamor against him made him seem great. Public protest is part of the power of every boss. So far, however, as I can gather, Butler was the leader of his organization, but only so long as he was a partisan politician; as he became a "boodler" pure and simple, he grew careless about his machine, and did his boodle business with the aid of the worst element of both parties. At any rate, the boodlers, and others as well, say that in later years he had about equal power with both parties, and he certainly was the ruler of St. Louis during the Republican administration of Ziegenhein, which was the worst in the history of the city. His method was to dictate enough of the candidates on both tickets to enable him, by selecting the worst from each, to elect the sort of men he required in his business. In other words, while honest Democrats and Republicans were "loyal to party" (a point of great pride with the idiots) and "voted straight," the Democratic boss and his Republican lieutenants decided what part of each ticket should be elected; then they sent around Butler's "Indians" (repeaters) by the van load to scratch ballots and "repeat" their votes, till the worst had made sure of the government by the worst, and Butler was in a position to do business.

His business was boodling, which is a more refined and a more dangerous form of corruption than the police blackmail of Minneapolis. It involves, not thieves, gamblers, and common women, but influential citizens, capitalists, and great corporations. For the stock-in-trade of the boodler is the rights, privileges, franchises, and real property of the city, and his source of corruption is the top, not the bottom, of society. Butler, thrown early in his career into contact with corporation managers, proved so useful to them that they introduced him to other financiers, and the scandal of his services attracted to him in due course all men who wanted things the city had to give. The boodlers told me that, according to the tradition of their combine, there "always was boodling in St. Louis."

Butler organized and systematized and developed it into a regular financial institution, and made it an integral part of the business community. He had for clients, regular or occasional, bankers and promoters; and the statements of boodlers, not yet on record, allege that every transportation and public convenience company that touches St. Louis had dealings with Butler's combine. And my best information is that these interests were not victims. Blackmail came in time, but in the beginning they originated the schemes of loot and started Butler on his career. Some interests paid him a regular salary, others a fee, and again he was a partner in the enterprise, with a special "rake-off" for his influence. "Fee" and "present" are his terms, and he has spoken openly of taking and giving them. I verily believe he regarded his charges as legitimate (he is the Croker type); but he knew that some people thought his services wrong. He once said that, when he had received his fee for a piece of legislation, he "went home and prayed that the measure might pass," and, he added facetiously, that "usually his prayers were answered."

His prayers were "usually answered" by the Municipal Assembly. This legislative body is divided into two houses—the upper, called the Council, consisting of thirteen members, elected at large; the lower, called the House of Delegates, with twenty-eight members, elected by wards; and each member of these bodies is paid twenty-five dollars a month salary by the city. With the mayor, this Assembly has practically complete control of all public property and valuable rights. Though Butler sometimes could rent or own the mayor, he preferred to be independent of him, so he formed in each part of the legislature a two-thirds majority—in the Council nine, in the House nineteen—which could pass bills over a veto. These were the "combines." They were regularly organized, and did their business under parliamentary rules. Each "combine" elected its chairman, who was elected chairman also of the legal bodies, where he appointed the committees, naming to each a majority of combine members.

In the early history of the combines, Butler's control was complete, because it was political. He picked the men who were to be legislators; they did as he bade them do, and the boodling was noiseless, safe, and moderate in price. Only wrongful acts were charged for, and a right once sold was good; for Butler kept his word. The definition of an honest man as one who will stay bought, fitted him. But it takes a very strong man to control himself and others when the money lust grows big, and it certainly grew big in St. Louis. Butler used to watch the downtown districts. He knew everybody, and when a railroad wanted a switch, or a financial house a franchise, Butler learned of it early. Sometimes he discovered the need and suggested it. Naming the regular price, say $10,000, he would tell the "boys" what was coming, and that there would be $1,000 to divide. He kept the rest, and the city got nothing. The bill was introduced and held up till Butler gave the word that the money was in hand; then it passed. As the business grew, however, not only illegitimate, but legitimate permissions were charged for, and at gradually increasing rates. Citizens who asked leave to make excavations in streets for any purpose, neighborhoods that had to have street lamps—all had to pay, and they did pay. In later years there was no other way. Business men who complained felt a certain pressure brought to bear on them from most unexpected quarters downtown.

A business man told me that a railroad which had a branch near his factory suggested that he go to the Municipal Legislature and get permission to have a switch run into his yard. He liked the idea, but when he found it would cost him eight or ten thousand dollars, he gave it up. Then the railroad became slow about handling his freight. He understood, and, being a fighter, he ferried the goods across the river to another road. That brought him the switch; and when he asked about it, the railroad man said:

"Oh, we got it done. You see, we pay a regular salary to some of those fellows, and they did it for us for nothing."

"Then why in the deuce did you send me to them?" asked the manufacturer.

"Well, you see," was the answer, "we like to keep in with them, and when we can throw them a little outside business we do."

In other words, a great railway corporation, not content with paying bribe salaries to these boodle aldermen, was ready, further to oblige them, to help coerce a manufacturer and a customer to go also and be blackmailed by the boodlers. "How can you buck a game like that?" this man asked me.

Very few tried to. Blackmail was all in the ordinary course of business, and the habit of submission became fixed—a habit of mind. The city itself was kept in darkness for weeks, pending the payment of $175,000 in bribes on the lighting contract, and complaining citizens went for light where Mayor Ziegenhein told them to go—to the moon.

Boodling was safe, and boodling was fat. Butler became rich and greedy, and neglectful of politics. Outside capital came in, and finding Butler bought, went over his head to the boodle combines. These creatures learned thus the value of franchises, and that Butler had been giving them an unduly small share of the boodle.

Then began a struggle, enormous in its vile melodrama,

for control of corruption—Butler to squeeze the municipal legislators and save his profits, they to wring from him their "fair share." Combines were formed within the old combines to make him pay more; and although he still was the legislative agent of the inner ring, he had to keep in his secret pay men who would argue for low rates, while the combine members, suspicious of one another, appointed their own legislative agent to meet Butler. Not sure even then, the cliques appointed "trailers" to follow their agent, watch him enter Butler's house, and then follow him to the place where the money was to be distributed. Charles A. Gutke and John K. Murrell represented Butler in the House of Delegates, Charles Kratz and Fred G. Uthoff in the Council. The other members suspected that these men got "something big on the side," so Butler had to hire a third to betray the combine to him. In the House, Robertson was the man. When Gutke had notified the chairman that a deal was on, and a meeting was called, the chairman would say:

"Gentlemen, the business before us to-night is [say] the Suburban Railway Bill. How much shall we ask for it?"

Gutke would move that "the price be $40,000." Some member of the outer ring would move $100,000 as fair boodle. The debate often waxed hot, and you hear of the drawing of revolvers. In this case (of the Suburban Railway) Robertson rose and moved a compromise of $75,000, urging moderation, lest they get nothing, and his price was carried. Then they would lobby over the appointment of the agent. They did not want Gutke, or anyone Butler owned, so they chose some other; and having adjourned, the outer ring would send a "trailer" to watch the agent, and sometimes a second "trailer" to watch the first.

They began to work up business on their own account, and, all decency gone, they sold out sometimes to both sides of a fight. The Central Traction deal in 1898 was an instance of this. Robert M. Snyder, a capitalist and promoter, of New York and Kansas City, came into St. Louis with a traction proposition inimical to the city railway interests. These felt secure. Through Butler they were paying seven members of the Council $5,000 a year each, but as a precaution John Scullin, Butler's associate, and one of the ablest capitalists of St. Louis, paid Councilman Uthoff a special retainer of $25,000 to watch the salaried boodlers. When Snyder found Butler and the combines against him, he set about buying the members individually, and, opening wine at his headquarters, began bidding for votes. This was the first break from Butler in a big deal, and caused great agitation among the boodlers. They did not go right over to Snyder; they saw Butler, and with Snyder's valuation of the franchise before them, made the boss go up to $175,000. Then the Council combine called a meeting in Gast's Garden to see if they could not agree on a price. Butler sent Uthoff there with instructions to cause a disagreement, or fix a price so high that Snyder would refuse to pay it. Uthoff obeyed, and, suggesting $25,000, persuaded some members to hold out for it, till the meeting broke up in a row. Then it was each man for himself, and all hurried to see Butler, and to see Snyder too. In the scramble various prices were paid. Four councilmen got from Snyder $10,000 each, one got $15,000, another $17,500, and one $50,000; twenty-five members of the House of Delegates got $3,000 each from him. In all, Snyder paid $250,000 for the franchise, and since Butler and his backers paid only $175,000 to beat it, the franchise was passed. Snyder turned around and sold it to his old opponents for $1,250,000. It was worth twice as much.

The man who received $50,000 from Snyder was the same Uthoff who had taken $25,000 from John Scullin, and his story as he has told it since on the stand is the most comical incident of the exposure. He says Snyder, with his "overcoat full of money," came out to his house to see him. They sat together on a sofa, and when Snyder was gone Uthoff found beside him a parcel containing $50,000. This he returned to the promoter, with the statement that he could not accept it, since he had already taken $25,000 from the other side; but he intimated that he could take $100,000. This Snyder promised, so Uthoff voted for the franchise.

The next day Butler called at Uthoff's house. Uthoff spoke first.

"I want to return this," he said, handing Butler the package of $25,000.

"That's what I came after," said Butler.

When Uthoff told this in the trial of Snyder, Snyder's counsel asked why he returned this $25,000.

"Because it wasn't mine," exclaimed Uthoff, flushing with anger. "I hadn't earned it."

But he believed he had earned the $100,000, and he besought Snyder for that sum, or, anyway, the $50,000. Snyder made him drink, and gave him just $5,000, taking by way of receipt a signed statement that the reports of bribery in connection with the Central Traction deal were utterly false; that "I [Uthoff] know you [Snyder] to be as far above offering a bribe as I am of taking one."

Irregular as all this was, however, the legislators kept up a pretense of partisanship and decency. In the debates arranged for in the combine caucus, a member or two were told off to make partisan speeches. Sometimes they were instructed to attack the combine, and one or two of the rascals used to take delight in arraigning their friends on the floor of the House, charging them with the exact facts.

But for the serious work no one knew his party. Butler had with him Republicans and Democrats, and there were Republicans and Democrats among those against him. He could trust none not in his special pay. He was the chief boodle broker and the legislature's best client; his political influence began to depend upon his boodling instead of the reverse.

He is a millionaire two or three times over now, but it is related that to someone who advised him to quit in time he replied that it wasn't a matter of money alone with him; he liked the business, and would rather make fifty dollars out of a switch than $500 in stocks. He enjoyed buying franchises cheap and selling them dear. In the lighting deal of 1899 Butler received $150,000, and paid out only $85,000—$47,500 to the House, $37,500 to the Council—and the haggling with the House combine caused those weeks of total darkness in the city. He had Gutke tell this combine that he could divide only $20,000 among them. They voted the measure, but, suspecting Butler of "holding out on them," moved to reconsider.

The citizens were furious, and a crowd went with ropes to the City Hall the night the motion to reconsider came up; but the combine was determined. Butler was there in person. He was more frightened than the delegates, and the sweat rolled down his face as he bargained with them. With the whole crowd looking on, and reporters so near that a delegate told me he expected to see the conversation in the papers the next morning, Butler threatened and pleaded, but finally promised to divide $47,500. That was an occasion for a burst of eloquence. The orators, indicating the citizens with ropes, declared that since it was plain the people wanted light, they would vote them light. And no doubt the people thought they had won, for it was not known till much later that the votes were bought by Butler, and that the citizens only hastened a corrupt bargain.

The next big boodle measure that Butler missed was the Suburban Traction, the same that led long after to disaster. This is the story Turner and Stock have been telling over and over in the boodle trials. Turner and his friends in the St. Louis Suburban Railway Company sought a franchise, for which they were willing to pay large bribes. Turner spoke about it to Butler, who said it would cost $145,000. This seemed too much, and Turner asked Stock to lobby the measure through. Stock managed it, but it cost him $144,000—$135,000 for the combine, $9,000 extra for Meysenburg—and then, before the money was paid over and the company in possession of its privilege, an injunction put a stop to all proceedings. The money was in safe-deposit vaults—$75,000 for the House combine in one, $60,000 for the Council combine in the other—and when the legislature adjourned, a long fight for the money ensued. Butler chuckled over the bungling. He is said to have drawn from it the lesson that "when you want a franchise, don't go to a novice for it; pay an expert, and he'll deliver the goods."

But the combine drew their own conclusions from it, and their moral was, that though boodling was a business by itself, it was a good business, and so easy that anybody could learn it by study. And study it they did. Two of them told me repeatedly that they traveled about the country looking up the business, and that a fellowship had grown up among boodling aldermen of the leading cities in the United States. Committees from Chicago would come to St. Louis to find out what "new games" the St. Louis boodlers had, and they gave the St. Louisans hints as to how they "did the business" in Chicago. So the Chicago and St. Louis boodlers used to visit Cleveland and Pittsburg and all the other cities, or, if the distance was too great, they got their ideas by those mysterious channels which run all through the "World of Graft." The meeting place in St. Louis was Decker's stable, and ideas unfolded there were developed into plans which, the boodlers say to-day, are only in abeyance. In Decker's stable the idea was born to sell the Union Market; and though the deal did not go through, the boodlers, when they saw it failing, made the market men pay $10,000 for killing it. This scheme is laid aside for the future. Another that failed was to sell the court-house, and this was well under way when it was discovered that the ground on which this public building stands was given to the city on condition that it was to be used for a court-house and nothing else.

But the grandest idea of all came from Philadelphia. In that city the gas-works were sold out to a private concern, and the water-works were to be sold next. The St. Louis fellows have been trying ever since to find a purchaser for their water-works. The plant is worth at least $40,000,000. But the boodlers thought they could let it go at $15,000,000, and get $1,000,000 or so themselves for the bargain. "The scheme was to do it and skip," said one of the boodlers who told me about it, "and if you could mix it all up with some filtering scheme it could be done; only some of us thought we could make more than $1,000,-

000 out of it—a fortune apiece. It will be done some day."

Such, then, is the boodling system as we see it in St. Louis. Everything the city owned was for sale by the officers elected by the people. The purchasers might be willing or unwilling takers; they might be citizens or outsiders; it was all one to the city government. So long as the members of the combines got the proceeds they would sell out the town. Would? They did and they will. If a city treasurer runs away with $50,000 there is a great halloo about it. In St. Louis the regularly organized thieves who rule have sold $50,000,000 worth of franchises and other valuable municipal assets. This is the estimate made for me by a banker, who said that the boodlers got not one-tenth of the value of the things they sold, but were content because they got it all themselves. And as to the future, my boodling informants said that all the possessions of the city were listed for future sale, that the list was in existence, and that the sale of these properties was only postponed on account of accident—the occurrence of Mr. Folk.

Preposterous? It certainly would seem so; but watch the people of St. Louis as I have, and as the boodlers have—then judge.

And remember, first, that Mr. Folk really was an accident. St. Louis knew in a general way, as other cities to-day know, what was going on, but there was no popular movement. Politicians named and elected him, and they expected no trouble from him. The moment he took office, on January 1, 1901, Butler called on him to appoint an organization man first assistant. When Folk refused, Butler could not understand it. Going away angry, he was back in three days to have his man appointed second assistant. The refusal of this also had some effect. The boodlers say Butler came out and bade them "Look out; I can't do anything with Folk, and I wouldn't wonder if he got after you." They took the warning; Butler did not. It seems never to have occurred to him that Mr. Folk would "get after" *him.*

What Butler felt, the public felt. When Mr. Folk took up, as he did immediately, election fraud cases, Butler called on him again, and told him which men he might not prosecute in earnest. The town laughed. When Butler was sent about his business, and Folk proceeded in earnest against the repeaters of both parties, even those who "had helped elect him," there was a sensation. But the stir was due to the novelty and the incomprehensibility of such non-partisan conduct in public office. Incredulous of honesty, St. Louis manifested the first signs of that faith in evil which is so characteristic of it. "Why didn't Mr. Folk take up boodling?" was the cynical challenge. "What do a few miserable repeaters amount to?"

Mr. Folk is a man of remarkable equanimity. When he has laid a course, he steers by it truly, and nothing can excite or divert him. He had said he would "do his duty," not that he would expose corruption or reform St. Louis; and beyond watching developments, he did nothing for a year to answer the public challenge. But he was making preparations. A civil lawyer, he was studying criminal law; and when, on January 23, 1902, he saw in the St. Louis *Star* a paragraph about the Suburban bribe fund in bank, he was ready. He sent out summonses by the wholesale for bankers, Suburban Railway officials and directors, legislators and politicians, and before the grand jury he examined them by the hour for days and days. Nobody knew anything; and though Mr. Folk was known to be "after the boodlers," those fellows and their friends were not alarmed and the public was not satisfied.

"Get indictments," was the challenge now. It was a "bluff"; but Mr. Folk took it up, and by a "bluff" he "got an indictment." And this is the way of it: the old row between the Suburban people and the boodle combine was going on in secret, but in a very bitter spirit. The money, lying in the safe-deposit vaults, in cash, was claimed by both parties. The boodlers said it was theirs because they had done their part by voting the franchise; the Suburban people said it was theirs because they had not obtained the franchise. The boodlers answered that the injunction against the franchise was not theirs, and they threatened to take the dispute before the grand jury. It was they who gave to a reporter a paragraph about the "boodle fund," and they meant to have it scare Turner and Stock. Stock really was "scared." When Mr. Folk's summons was served on him, he believed the boodlers had "squealed," and he fainted. The deputy who saw the effect of the summons told Mr. Folk, who, seeing in it only evidence of weakness and guilt, sent for the lawyer who represented Stock and Turner, and boldly gave him the choice for his clients of being witnesses or defendants. The lawyer was firm, but Folk advised him to consult his clients, and their choice was to be witnesses. Their confession and the seizure of the bribe fund in escrow gave Folk the whole inside story of the Suburban deal, and evidence in plenty for indictments. He took seven, and the reputation and standing of the first culprits showed right away not only the fearlessness of the prosecution, but the variety and power and wealth of the St. Louis species of boodler. There was Charles Kratz, agent of the Council combine; John K. Murrell, agent of the House combine; Emil A. Meysenburg, councilman and "good citizen"—all for taking bribes; Ellis Wainwright and Henry Nicolaus, millionaire brewers, and directors of the Suburban Railway Company for bribery; and Julius Lehmann and Henry A. Faulkner, of the House combine, for perjury. This news caused consternation; but the ring rallied, held together, and the cynics said, "They never will be tried."

The outlook was stormy. Mr. Folk felt now in full force the powerful interests that opposed him. The standing of some of the prisoners was one thing; another was the character of the men who went on their bail bond—Butler for the bribe takers, other millionaires for the bribers. But most serious was the flow of persons who went to Mr. Folk privately and besought or bade him desist; they were not alone politicians, but solid, innocent business men, eminent lawyers, and good friends. Hardly a man he knew but came to him at one time or another, in one way or another, to plead for some rascal or other. Threats of assassination and political ruin, offers of political promotion and of remunerative and legitimate partnerships, veiled bribes—everything he might fear was held up on one side, everything he might want on the other. "When you are doing a thing like this," he says now, "you cannot listen to anybody; you have to think for yourself and rely on yourself alone. I knew I simply had to succeed; and, success or failure, I felt that a political future was not to be considered, so I shut out all idea of it."

So he went on silently but surely; how surely may be inferred from the fact that in all his dealings with witnesses who turned State's evidence he has not made one misstep; there have been no misunderstandings, and no charges against him of foul play. While the pressure from behind never ceased, and the defiance before him was bold, "Go higher up" was the challenge. He was going higher up. With confessions of Turner and Stock, and the indictments for perjury for examples, he re-examined witnesses; and though the big men were furnishing the little boodlers with legal advice and drilling them in their stories, there were breaks here and there. The story of the Central Traction deal began to develop, and that went higher up, straight into the group of millionaires led by Butler.

But there was an impassable barrier in the law on bribery. American legislators do not legislate harshly against their chief vice. The State of Missouri limits the liability of a briber to three years, and the Traction deal was outlawed for most of the principals in it. But the law excepted non-residents, and Mr. Folk found that in moments of vanity Robert M. Snyder had described himself as "of New York," so he had Snyder indicted for bribery, and George J. Kobusch, president of the St. Louis Car Company, for perjury, Kobusch having sworn that he knew of no bribery for the Central Traction franchise, when he himself had paid out money. Kobusch turned State's witness against Snyder.

High as these indictments were, the cry for Butler persisted, and the skeptical tone of it made it plain that to break up the ring Mr. Folk had to catch the boss. And he did catch him. Saved by missing the Suburban business, saved by the law in the Central Traction affair, Butler lost by his temerity; he went on boodling after Mr. Folk was in office. He offered "presents" of $2,500 each to the two medical members of the Health Board for their approval of a garbage contract which was to net him

$232,500. So the "Old Man," the head of the boodlers, and the legislative agent of the financial district, was indicted.

But the ring did not part, and the public faith in evil remained steadfast. No one had been tried. The trials were approaching, and the understanding was that the first of them was to be made a test. A defeat might stop Mr. Folk, and he realized the moral effect such a result would have. But he was sure of his cases against Murrell and Kratz, and if he convicted them the way was open to both combines and to the big men behind them. To all appearances these men also were confident, and with the lawyers engaged for them they might well have been. Suddenly it was decided that Murrell was weak, and might "cave." He ran away. The shock of this to the community is hard to realize now. It was the first public proof of guilt, and the first break in the ring of little boodlers. To Mr. Folk it was the first serious check, for he could not now indict the House combine. Then, too, Kratz was in Florida, and the Circuit Attorney saw himself going into court with the weakest of his early cases, that of Meysenburg. In genuine alarm he moved heavy increases in the bail bonds. All the lawyers in all the cases combined to defeat this move, and the fight lasted for days; but Mr. Folk won. Kratz returned in a rage to find bail. With his connections and his property he could give any amount, he boasted, and he offered $100,000. In spite of the protest of the counsel engaged for him, he insisted upon furnishing $20,000, and he denounced the effort to discredit him with the insinuation that such as he would avoid trial. He even asked to be tried first, but wiser heads on his side chose the Meysenburg case.

The weakness of this case lay in the indirection of the

bribe. Meysenburg, a business man of repute, took for his vote on the Suburban franchise, not money; he sold for $9,000 some two hundred shares of worthless stock. This might be made to look like a regular business transaction, and half a dozen of the best lawyers in the State appeared to press that view. Mr. Folk, however, met these lawyers point by point, and point by point he beat them all, displaying a knowledge of law which astounded them, and an attitude toward the prisoner which won the jury, and might well reform the methods of haranguing prosecutors all over this country. Naturally without malice, he is impersonal; he did not attack the prisoner. He was not there for that purpose. He was defending the State, not prosecuting the individual. "The defendant is a mere atom," he tells his juries; "if we could enforce the law without punishing individuals, we should not be here; but we cannot. Only by making an example of the criminal can we prevent crime. And as to the prisoner, he cannot complain, because his own deeds are his doomsmen." At one stage of the Faulkner trial, when ex-Governor Johnson was talking about the rights of the prisoner, Mr. Folk remarked that the State had rights also. "Oh, d—— the rights of the State!" was the retort, and the jury heard it. Many juries have heard this view. One of the permanent services Mr. Folk has rendered is to impress upon the minds, not only of juries, but of the people generally, and in particular upon the Courts of Appeal (which often forget it), that while the criminal law has been developed into a great machine to preserve the rights, and much more, of the criminal, the rights of the State also should be guarded.

Meysenburg was found guilty and sentenced to three years. The man was shocked limp, and the ring broke.

Kratz ran away. He was advised to go, and, like Murrell, he had promises of plenty of money; unlike Murrell, however, Kratz stood on the order of his going. He made the big fellows give him a large sum of cash, and for the fulfillment of their promise of more he waited menacingly in New Orleans. Supplied there with all he demanded, this Council leader stepped across into Mexico, and has gone into business there on a large scale. With Kratz safely away, the ring was nerved up again, and Meysenburg appeared in court with five well-known millionaires to give an appeal bond of $25,000. "I could have got more," he told the reporters, "but I guess that's enough."

With the way to both boodle combines closed thus by the flight of their go-betweens, Mr. Folk might well have been stayed; but he wasn't. He proceeded with his examination of witnesses, and to loosen their tongues he brought on the trials of Lehmann and Faulkner for perjury. They were well defended, but against them appeared, as against Meysenburg, President Turner, of the Suburban Railway, and Philip Stock, the brewery secretary. The perjurers were found guilty. Meanwhile Mr. Folk was trying through both Washington and Jefferson City to have Murrell and Kratz brought back. These regular channels failing, he applied to his sources of information in Murrell's (the House) combine, and he soon learned that the fugitive was ill, without money, and unable to communicate with his wife or friends. Money that had been raised for him to flee with had been taken by others, and another fund sent to him by a fellow-boodler did not reach him. The fellow-boodler did, but he failed to deliver the money. Murrell wanted to come home, and Mr. Folk, glad to welcome him, let him come as far as a small town just outside of St. Louis. There he was held till Mr. Folk could arrange a *coup* and make sure of a witness to corroborate what Murrell should say; for, secure in the absence of Murrell, the whole House combine was denying everything. One day (in September, 1902) Mr. Folk called one of them, George F. Robertson, into his office.

They had a long talk together, and Mr. Folk asked him, as he had time and again, to tell what he knew about the Suburban deal.

"I have told you many times, Mr. Folk," said Robertson, "that I know nothing about that."

"What would you say if you should see Murrell here?" Mr. Folk asked.

"Murrell!" exclaimed Robertson. "That's good, that is. Why, yes, I'd like to see Murrell."

He was laughing as Mr. Folk went to the door and called, "Murrell." Murrell walked in. Robertson's smile passed. He gripped his seat, and arose like a man lifted by an electric shock. Once on his feet, he stood there staring as at a ghost.

"Murrell," said Mr. Folk quietly, "the jig is up, isn't it?"

"Yes," said Murrell, "it's all up."

"You've told everything?"

"Everything."

Robertson sank into his chair. When he had time to recover his self-control, Mr. Folk asked him if he was ready to talk about the Suburban deal.

"Well, I don't see what else I can do, Mr. Folk; you've got me."

Robertson told all, and, with Murrell and Turner and Stock and the rolls of money to support him, Mr. Folk indicted for bribery or perjury, or both, the remaining members of the House combine, sixteen men at one swoop. Some escaped. One, Charles Kelly, a leading witness in another case, fled to Europe with more money than anyone believed he owned, and he returned after a high time with plenty left. A leading financier of Missouri went away at about the same time, and when he got back, at about the same time with Kelly, the statute of limitation in the financier's case covered them both.

With all his success these losses were made the most of; it was remarked that Mr. Folk had not yet convicted a very rich man. The Snyder case was coming up, and with it a chance to show that even the power of money was not irresistible. Snyder, now a banker in Kansas City, did not deny or attempt to disprove the charges of bribery; he made his defense his claim to continuous residence in the State. Mr. Folk was not taken unawares; he proved the bribery and he proved the non-residence too, and the banker was sentenced to five years' imprisonment.

One other trial intervened, that of Edmund Bersch of the House combine, and he was convicted of bribery and perjury. But all interest centered now in the trial of Edward Butler, the boss, who, the people said, would not be indicted; who, indicted, they said, would never be tried. Now they were saying he would never be convicted.

When Boss Tweed was tried in New York, his power was broken, his machine smashed, his money spent, and the people were worked up to a fury against him. The most eminent members of the New York bar prosecuted him. The most eminent members of the St. Louis Bar were engaged to defend Butler. He was still the boss, he had millions of his own, and back of him were the resources, financial and political, of the leading men of St. Louis. That the people were against him appeared in only one sign, that of the special juries, carefully chosen to keep out men privately known to be implicated. These juries had invariably convicted the boodlers. Butler asked to be tried in some other town. Mr. Folk suggested Columbia, the university town of the State of Missouri.

Columbia was chosen, and Butler's sons went up there with their heelers to "fix the town." They spent money freely, and because the loafers drank with them plentifully, the Butlerites thought they "had the town right." But they did not know Columbia; neither did Butler. When he stepped off the train, he asked genially what the business of the town was.

"Education," was the answer.

"Education!" he blurted. "That's a h—l of a business!" And he conducted himself as if he did not understand what it meant. His friends having prepared the way for a "good fellow," Butler set about proving himself such, and his reception in the bar-rooms and streets was so flattering that it was predicted in his crowd that Folk would never leave Columbia alive. But Mr. Folk understood the people better. Stanch as the leading interests of St. Louis were against him, he always held that his unflinching juries meant that the silent people of St. Louis were against boodlers and out in the State he felt still surer of this. He was right. There was no demonstration for him. He was welcomed, but in decorous fashion; and all he saw by way of prejudice was the friendly look out of kind eyes that went with the warm pressure of strange hands. When the jury was drawn, every man on it proved to be a Democrat, and three were members of the Democratic County Committee. Mr. Folk was urged to challenge these, for, after all, Colonel Butler was at the head of their machine. He accepted them. He might as well have objected to the judge, John A. Hockaday, who also was a Democrat. "No, sir," said Mr. Folk; "I am a Democrat, and I will try Butler before a Democratic judge and a Democratic jury."

The trial was a scene to save out of all the hideousness before and after it. The little old court-house headed one end of a short main street, the university the other; farmers' mule teams were hitched all along between. From far and near people came to see this trial, and, with the significance of it in mind, men halted to read over the entrance to the court these words, chiseled long ago: "Oh, Justice, when driven from other habitations, make this thy dwelling-place." You could see the appropriateness of that legend take hold of men, and in the spirit of it they passed into the dingy courtroom. There the rows of intent faces seemed to express that same sentiment. The jury looked, the judge personified it. He alone was cold, but he was attentive, deliberate, and reasonable; you were sure of his common sense; you understood his rulings; and of his uprightness you were convinced by the way he seemed to lean, just a little, toward the prisoner. I don't believe they will find any errors, however trivial, on which to reverse John A. Hockaday.* Even the prosecutor was fair. It was not Edward Butler who was on trial, it was the State; and never before did Mr. Folk plead so earnestly for this conception of his work. Outside, in the churches, prayer-meetings were held. These were private and undemonstrative; the praying citizens did not tell even Mr. Folk that they were asking their God to give him strength. Indirectly it came to him, and, first fine sign as it was of approval from his client, the people, it moved him deeply. And when, the

* See *Post Scriptum*, end of chapter.

plain case plainly stated, he made his final appeal to the jury, the address was a statement of the impersonal significance of the evidence, and of the State's need of patriotic service and defense. "Missouri, Missouri," he said softly, with simple, convincing sincerity, "I am pleading for thee, pleading for thee." And the jury understood. The judge was only clear and fair, but the twelve men took his instructions out with them, and when they came back their verdict was, "Guilty; three years."

That was Missouri. What of St. Louis? Some years ago, when Butler was young in corruption, he was caught gambling, and with the charge pending against him St. Louis rose to challenge him. Meetings were held all over the city—one in the Exchange downtown—to denounce the political leader, who, an offense always, had dared commit the felony of gambling. Now, when he was caught and convicted and sentenced for bribery, what did St. Louis do? The first comment I heard in the streets when we all got back that day was that "Butler would never wear the stripes." I heard it time and again, and you can hear it from banker and barber there to-day. Butler himself behaved decently. He stayed indoors for a few weeks—till a committee of citizens from the best residence section called upon him to come forth and put through the House of Delegates a bill for the improvement of a street in their neighborhood; and Butler had this done!

One of the first greetings to Mr. Folk was a warning from a high source that now at length he had gone far enough, and on the heels of this came an order from the Police Department that hereafter all communications from him to the police should be made in writing. This meant slow arrests; it meant that the fight was to go on. Well, Mr. Folk had meant to go on, anyway.

"Officer," he said to the man who brought the message, "go back to the man who sent you, and say to him that I understand him, and that hereafter all my communications with his department will be in the form of *indictments.*"

That department retreated in haste, explaining and apologizing, and offering all possible facilities. Mr. Folk went on with his business. He put on trial Henry Nicolaus, the brewer, accused of bribery. Mr. Nicolaus pleaded that he did not know what was to be the use of a note for $140,000 which he had endorsed. And on this the judge took the case away from the jury and directed a verdict of not guilty. It was the first case Mr. Folk had lost. He won the next eight, all boodle legislators, making his record fourteen against one. But the Supreme Court, technical and slow, is the last stand for such criminals, and they won their first fight there.* The Meysenburg case was sent back for retrial.

Mr. Folk has work ahead of him for the two years remaining of his term, and he is the man to carry it all through. But where is it all to end? There are more men to be indicted, many more to be tried, and there is much more corruption to be disclosed. But the people of St. Louis know enough. What are they going to do about it?

They have had one opportunity already to act. In November (1902), just before the Butler verdict, but after the trial was begun, there was an election. Some of the offices to be filled might have to do with boodling cases. Mr. Folk and boodling were the natural issue, but the politicians avoided it. Neither party "claimed" Mr. Folk. Both parties took counsel of Butler in making up their

* See *Post Scriptum,* end of chapter.

tickets, and they satisfied him. The Democrats did not mention Folk's name in the platform, and they nominated Butler's son for the seat in Congress from which he had repeatedly been ousted for fraud at the polls.

"Why?" I asked a Democratic leader, who said he controlled all but four districts in his organization.

"Because I needed those Butler districts," he answered.

"But isn't there enough anti-boodling sentiment in this town to offset those districts?"

"I don't think so."

Perhaps he was right. And yet those juries and those prayers must mean something.

Mr. Folk says, "Ninety-nine per cent. of the people are honest; only one per cent. is dishonest. But the one per cent. is perniciously active." In other words, the people are sound, but without leaders. Another official, of irreproachable character himself, said that the trouble was there was "no one fit to throw the first stone."

However this may be, here are the facts:

In the midst of all these sensations, and this obvious, obstinate political rottenness, the innocent citizens, who must be at least a decisive minority, did not register last fall. Butler, the papers said, had great furniture vans going about with men who were said to be repeaters, and yet the registration was the lowest in many years. When the Butlerized tickets were announced, there was no audible protest. It was the time for an independent movement. A third ticket might not have won, but it would have shown the politicians (whether they counted them in or out) how many honest votes there were in the city, and what they would have to reckon with in the force of public sentiment. Nothing of the sort was done. St. Louis, rich, dirty, and despoiled, was busy with business.

Another opportunity is coming soon. In April the city votes for municipal legislators, and since the municipal assembly has been the scene of most of the corruption, you would think boodling would surely be an issue then. I doubt it. When I was there in January (1903), the politicians were planning to keep it out, and their ingenious scheme was to combine on one ticket; that is to say, each group of leaders would name half the nominees, who were to be put on identical tickets, making no contest at all. And to avoid suspicion, these nominations were to be exceptionally, yes, "remarkably good." *

That is the old Butler non-partisan or bi-partisan system. It emanates now from the rich men back of the ring, but it means that the ring is intact, alert, and hopeful. They are "playing for time." The convicts sitting in the municipal assembly, the convicts appealing to the higher courts, the rich men abroad, the bankers down town—all are waiting for something. What are they waiting for?

Charles Kratz, the ex-president of the Council, head and go-between of the Council combine, the fugitive from justice, who, by his flight, blocks the way to the exposure and conviction of the rich and influential men who are holding the people of Missouri in check and keeping boodling from going before the people as a political issue, this criminal exile, thus backed, was asked this question in Mexico, and here is the answer he returned:

"I am waiting for Joe Folk's term to expire. Then I am going home to run for Governor of Missouri and vindication."

* See *Post Scriptum,* end of chapter.

Post Scriptum, December, 1904.—The tickets were not "remarkably good." "Boodle" was not in the platform, nor "reform." The bi-partisan boodlers, with reformers and "respectable" business men for backers, faced it out, and Boss Butler reorganized the new House of Delegates with his man for Speaker and the superintendent of his garbage plant (in the interest of which he offered the bribes for which he was convicted) for chairman of the Sanitary Committee.

And the Supreme Court of Missouri reversed his case and all the other boodle cases one by one, then by wholesale. The whole machinery of justice broke down under the strain of boodle pull.

Meanwhile, however, Mr. Folk uncovered corruption in the State and, announcing himself a candidate for Governor, has appealed from the Court to the People, from the City of St. Louis to the State of Missouri.

Pittsburg: A City Ashamed

(*May, 1903*)

Minneapolis was an example of police corruption; St. Louis of financial corruption. Pittsburg is an example of both police and financial corruption. The two other cities have found each an official who has exposed them. Pittsburg has had no such man and no exposure. The city has been described physically as "Hell with the lid off"; politically it is hell with the lid on. I am not going to lift the lid. The exposition of what the people know and stand is the purpose of these articles, not the exposure of corruption, and the exposure of Pittsburg is not necessary. There are earnest men in the town who declare it must blow up of itself soon. I doubt that; but even if it does burst, the people of Pittsburg will learn little more than they know now. It is not ignorance that keeps American citizens subservient; neither is it indifference. The Pittsburgers know, and a strong minority of them care; they have risen against their ring and beaten it, only to look about and find another ring around them. Angry and ashamed, Pittsburg is a type of the city that has tried to be free and failed.

A sturdy city it is, too, the second in Pennsylvania. Two rivers flow past it to make a third, the Ohio, in front, and all around and beneath it are natural gas and coal which feed a thousand furnaces that smoke all day and flame all night to make Pittsburg the Birmingham of America. Rich in natural resources, it is richest in the quality of its population. Six days and six nights these people labor, molding iron and forging steel, and they are not tired; on the seventh day they rest, because that is the Sabbath. They are Scotch Presbyterians and Protestant Irish. This stock had an actual majority not many years ago, and now, though the population has grown to 354,000 in Pittsburg proper (counting Allegheny across the river, 130,000, and other communities, politically separate, but essentially integral parts of the proposed Greater Pittsburg, the total is 750,000), the Scotch and Scotch-Irish still predominate, and their clean, strong faces characterize the crowds in the streets. Canny, busy, and brave, they built up their city almost in secret, making millions and hardly mentioning it. Not till outsiders came in to buy some of them out did the world (and Pittsburg and some of the millionaires in it) discover that the Iron City had been making not only steel and glass, but multi-millionaires. A banker told a business man as a secret one day about three years ago that within six months a "bunch of about a hundred new millionaires would be born in Pittsburg," and the births happened on time. And more beside. But even the bloom of millions did not hurt the city. Pittsburg is an unpretentious, prosperous city of tremendous industry and healthy, steady men.

Superior as it is in some other respects, however, Scotch-Irish Pittsburg, politically, is no better than Irish New York or Scandinavian Minneapolis, and little better than German St. Louis. These people, like any other strain of the free American, have despoiled the government—despoiled it, let it be despoiled, and bowed to the despoiling boss. There is nothing in the un-American excuse that this or that foreign nationality has prostituted "our great and glorious institutions." We all do it, all breeds alike. And there is nothing in the complaint that the lower elements of our city populations are the source of our disgrace. In St. Louis corruption came from the top, in Minneapolis from the bottom. In Pittsburg it comes from both extremities, but it began above.

The railroads began the corruption of this city. There "always was some dishonesty," as the oldest public men I talked with said, but it was occasional and criminal till the first great corporation made it business-like and respectable. The municipality issued bonds to help the infant railroads to develop the city, and, as in so many American cities, the roads repudiated the debt and interest, and went into politics. The Pennsylvania Railroad was in the system from the start, and, as the other roads came in and found the city government bought up by those before them, they purchased their rights of way by outbribing the older roads, then joined the ring to acquire more rights for themselves and to keep belated rivals out. As corporations multiplied and capital branched out, corruption increased naturally, but the notable characteristic of the "Pittsburg plan" of misgovernment was that it was not a haphazard growth, but a deliberate, intelligent organization. It was conceived in one mind, built up by one will, and this master spirit ruled, not like Croker in New York, a solid majority; nor like Butler in St. Louis, a bipartisan minority; but the whole town—financial, commercial, and political. The boss of Pittsburg was Christopher L. Magee, a great man, and when he died he was regarded by many of the strongest men in Pittsburg as their leading citizen.

"Chris," as he was called, was a charming character. I have seen Pittsburgers grow black in the face denouncing his ring, but when I asked, "What kind of a man was Magee?" they would cool and say, "Chris? Chris was one of the best men God ever made." If I smiled, they would say, "That is all right. You smile, and you can go ahead and show up the ring. You may describe this town as the worst in the country. But you get Magee wrong and you'll have all Pittsburg up in arms." Then they would tell me that "Magee robbed the town," or, perhaps, they would speak of the fund raising to erect a monument to the dead boss.

So I must be careful. And, to begin with, Magee did not, technically speaking, rob the town. That was not his way, and it would be a carelessly unnecessary way in Pennsylvania. But surely he does not deserve a monument.

Magee was an American. His paternal great-grandfather served in the Revolution, and settled in Pittsburg at the close of the war. Christopher was born on Good Friday, April 14, 1848. He was sent to school till he was fifteen years old. Then his father died, and "Squire" or "Tommy" Steele, his uncle, a boss of that day, gave him his start in life with a place in the City Treasury. When just twenty-one, he made him cashier, and two years later

Chris had himself elected City Treasurer by a majority of 1100 on a ticket the head of which was beaten by 1500 votes.

Such was his popularity; and, though he systematized and capitalized it, it lasted to the end, for the foundation thereof was goodness of heart and personal charm. Magee was tall, strong, and gracefully built. His hair was dark till it turned gray, then his short mustache and his eyebrows held black, and his face expressed easily sure power and genial, hearty kindness. But he was ambitious for power, and all his goodness of heart was directed by a shrewd mind.

When Chris saw the natural following gathering about him he realized, young as he was, the use of it, and he retired from office (holding only a fire commissionership) with the avowed purpose of becoming a boss. Determined to make his ring perfect, he went to Philadelphia to study the plan in operation there. Later, when the Tweed ring was broken, he spent months in New York looking into Tammany's machine methods and the mistakes which had led to its exposure and disruption. With that cheerful candor which softens indignation he told a fellow-townsman (who told me) what he was doing in New York; and when Magee returned he reported that a ring could be made as safe as a bank. He had, to start with, a growing town too busy for self-government; two not very unequal parties, neither of them well organized; a clear field in his own, the majority party in the city, county, and State. There was boodle, but it was loosely shared by too many persons. The governing instrument was the old charter of 1816, which lodged all the powers—legislative, administrative, and executive—in the councils, common and select. The mayor was a peace officer, with no responsible power. Indeed, there was no responsibility anywhere. There were no departments. Committees of councils did the work usually done by departments, and the councilmen, unsalaried and unanswerable individually, were organized into what might have become a combine had not Magee set about establishing the one-man power there.

To control councils Magee had to organize the wards, and he was managing this successfully at the primaries, when a new and an important figure appeared on the scene—William Flinn. Flinn was Irish, a Protestant of Catholic stock, a boss contractor, and a natural politician. He beat one of Magee's brothers in his ward. Magee laughed, inquired, and, finding him a man of opposite or complementary disposition and talents, took him into a partnership. A happy, profitable combination, it lasted for life. Magee wanted power, Flinn wealth. Each got both these things; but Magee spent his wealth for more power, and Flinn spent his power for more wealth. Magee was the sower, Flinn the reaper. In dealing with men they came to be necessary to each other, these two. Magee attracted followers, Flinn employed them. The men Magee won Flinn compelled to obey, and those he lost Magee won back. When the councils were first under his control Magee stood in the lobby to direct them, always by suggestions and requests, which sometimes a mean and ungrateful fellow would say he could not heed. Magee told him it was all right, which saved the man, but lost the vote. So Flinn took the lobby post, and he said: "Here, you go and vote aye." If they disobeyed the plain order Flinn punished them, and so harshly that they would run to Magee to complain. He comforted them. "Never mind Flinn," he would say sympathetically; "he gives me no end of trouble, too. But I'd like to have you do what he asked. Go and do it for me, and let me attend to Flinn. I'll fix him."

Magee could command, too, and fight and punish. If he had been alone he probably would have hardened with years. And so Flinn, after Magee died, softened with time, but too late. He was useful to Magee, Magee was indispensable to him. Molasses and vinegar, diplomacy and force, mind and will, they were well mated. But Magee was the genius. It was Magee that laid the plans they worked out together.

Boss Magee's idea was not to corrupt the city government, but to be it; not to hire votes in councils, but to own councilmen; and so, having seized control of his organization, he nominated cheap or dependent men for the select and common councils. Relatives and friends were his first recourse, then came bartenders, saloonkeepers, liquor dealers, and others allied to the vices, who were subject to police regulation and dependent in a business way upon the maladministration of law. For the rest he preferred men who had no visible means of support, and to maintain them he used the usual means—patronage. And to make his dependents secure he took over the county government. Pittsburg is in Allegheny County, which has always been more strongly Republican than the city. No matter what happened in the city, the county pay-roll was always Magee's, and he made the county part of the city government.

With all this city and county patronage at his command, Magee went deliberately about undermining the Democratic party. The minority organization is useful to a majority leader; it saves him trouble and worry in ordinary times; in party crises he can use it to whip his own followers into line; and when the people of a city rise in revolt it is essential for absolute rule that you have the power not only to prevent the minority leaders from combining with the good citizens, but to unite the two organizations to whip the community into shape. Moreover, the existence of a supposed opposition party splits the independent vote and helps to keep alive that sentiment, "loyalty to party," which is one of the best holds the boss has on his unruly subjects. All bosses, as we have seen in Minneapolis and St. Louis, rise above partisan bias. Magee, the wisest of them, was also the most generous, and he liked to win over opponents who were useful to him. Whenever he heard of an able Democratic worker in a ward, he sent for his own Republican leader. "So-and-so is a good man, isn't he?" he would ask. "Going to give you a run, isn't he? Find out what he wants, and we'll see what we can do. We must have him." Thus the able Democrat achieved office for himself or his friend, and the city or the county paid. At one time, I was told, nearly one-quarter of the places on the pay-roll were held by Democrats, who were, of course, grateful to Chris Magee, and enabled him in emergencies to wield their influence against revolting Republicans. Many a time a subservient Democrat got Republican votes to beat a "dangerous" Republican, and when Magee, toward the end of his career, wished to go to the State Senate, both parties united in his nomination and elected him unanimously.

Business men came almost as cheap as politicians, and they came also at the city's expense. Magee had control of public funds and the choice of depositories. That is enough for the average banker—not only for him that is chosen, but for him also that may some day hope to be chosen—and Magee dealt with the best of those in Pittsburg. This service, moreover, not only kept them docile, but gave him and Flinn credit at their banks. Then, too, Flinn and Magee's operations soon developed on a scale which made their business attractive to the largest financial institutions for the profits on their loans, and thus enabled them to distribute and share in the golden opportunities of big deals. There are ring banks in Pittsburg, ring trust companies, and ring brokers. The manufacturers and the merchants were kept well in hand by many little municipal grants and privileges, such as switches, wharf rights, and street and alley vacations. These street vacations are a tremendous power in most cities. A foundry occupies a block, spreads to the next block, and wants the street between. In St. Louis the business man boodled for his street. In Pittsburg he went to Magee, and I have heard such a man praise Chris, "because when I called on him his outer office was filled with waiting politicians, but he knew I was a business man and in a hurry; he called me in first, and he gave me the street without any fuss. I tell you it was a sad day for Pittsburg when Chris Magee died." This business man, the typical American merchant everywhere, cares no more for his city's interest than the politician does, and there is more light on American political corruption in such a speech than in the most sensational exposure of details. The business men of Pittsburg paid for their little favors in "contributions to the campaign fund," plus the loss of their self-respect, the liberty of the citizens generally, and (this may appeal to their mean souls) in higher taxes.

As for the railroads, they did not have to be bought or driven in; they came, and promptly, too. The Pennsylvania appeared early, just behind Magee, who handled their passes and looked out for their interest in councils and afterwards at the State Legislature. The Pennsylvania passes, especially those to Atlantic City and Harrisburg, have always been a "great graft" in Pittsburg. For the sort of men Magee had to control a pass had a value above the price of a ticket; to "flash" one is to show a badge of power and relationship to the ring. The big ringsters, of course, got from the railroads financial help when cornered in business deals—stock tips, shares in speculative and other financial turns, and political support. The Pennsylvania Railroad is a power in Pennsylvania politics, it is part of the State ring, and part also of the Pittsburg ring. The city paid in all sorts of rights and privileges, streets, bridges, etc., and in certain periods the business interests of the city were sacrificed to leave the Pennsylvania Road in exclusive control of a freight traffic it could not handle alone.

With the city, the county, the Republican and Democratic organizations, the railroads and other corporations, the financiers and the business men, all well under control, Magee needed only the State to make his rule absolute. And he was entitled to it. In a State like New York, where one party controls the Legislature and another the city, the people in the cities may expect some protection from party opposition. In Pennsylvania, where the Republicans have an overwhelming majority, the Legislature at Harrisburg is an essential part of the government of Pennsylvania cities, and that is ruled by a State ring. Magee's ring was a link in the State ring, and it was no more than right that the State ring should become a link in his ring. The arrangement was easily made. One man, Matthew S. Quay, had received from the people all the power in the State, and Magee saw Quay. They came to an understanding without the least trouble. Flinn was to be in the Senate, Magee in the lobby, and they were to give unto Quay political support for his business in the State in return for his surrender to them of the State's functions of legislation for the city of Pittsburg.

Now such understandings are common in our politics, but they are verbal usually and pretty well kept, and this of Magee and Quay was also founded in secret good faith. But Quay, in crises, has a way of straining points to win, and there were no limits to Magee's ambition for power. Quay and Magee quarreled constantly over the division of powers and spoils, so after a few years of squabbling they reduced their agreement to writing. This precious instrument has never been published. But the agreement was broken in a great row once, and when William Flinn and J. O. Brown undertook to settle the differences and renew the bond, Flinn wrote out in pencil in his own hand an amended duplicate which he submitted to Quay, whose son subsequently gave it out for publication. A facsimile of one page is reproduced in this article. Here is the whole contract, with all the unconscious humor of the "party of the first part" and "said party of the second part," a political-legal-commercial insult to a people boastful of self-government:

"Memorandum and agreement between M. S. Quay of the first part and J. O. Brown and William Flinn of the second part, the consideration of this agreement being the mutual political and business advantage which may result therefrom.

"First—The said M. S. Quay is to have the benefit of the influence in all matters in state and national politics of the said parties of the second part, the said parties agreeing that they will secure the election of delegates to the state and national convention, who will be guided in all matters by the wishes of the said party of the first part, and who will also secure the election of members of the state senate from the

Forty-third, Forty-fourth, and Forty-fifth senatorial districts, and also secure the election of members of the house of representatives south of the Monongahela and Ohio rivers in the county of Allegheny, who will be guided by the wishes and request of the said party of the first part during the continuance of this agreement upon all political matters. The different candidates for the various positions mentioned shall be selected by the parties of the second part, and all the positions of state and national appointments made in this territory mentioned shall be satisfactory to and secure the indorsement of the party of the second part, when the appointment is made either by or through the party of the first part, or his friends or political associates. All legislation affecting the parties of the second part, affecting cities of the second class, shall receive the hearty co-operation and assistance of the party of the first part, and legislation which may affect their business shall likewise receive the hearty co-operation and help of the party of the first part. It being distinctly understood that at the approaching national convention, to be held at St. Louis, the delegates from the Twenty-second congressional district shall neither by voice nor vote do other than what is satisfactory to the party of the first part. The party of the first part agrees to use his influence and secure the support of his friends and political associates to support the Republican county and city ticket, when nominated, both in the city of Pittsburg and Allegheny, and the county of Allegheny, and that he will discountenance the factional fighting by his friends and associates for county offices during the continuation of this agreement. This agreement is not to be binding upon the parties of the second part when a candidate for any office who [*sic*] shall reside in Allegheny county, and shall only be binding if the party of the first part is a candidate for United States senator to succeed himself so far as this office is concerned. In the Forty-third senatorial district a new senator shall be elected to succeed Senator Upperman. In the Forty-fifth senatorial district the party of the first part shall secure

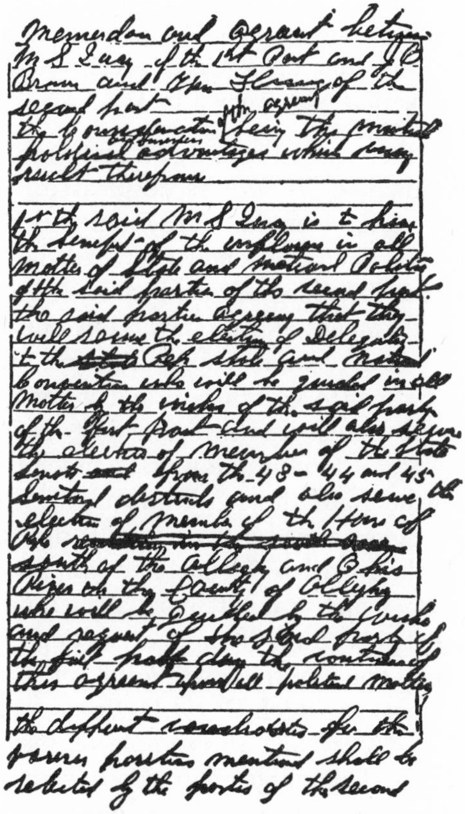

Memerandum and agreemt between
M S Quay of the 1st Part and J O
Brown and Wm Flinn of the
second part
the consideration of this agreemt being the mutual
political advantages which may
result therefrom

1st the said M S Quay is to have
the benefit of the influence in all
matters of State and national Politics
of the said parties of the second part.
the said parties agreeing that they
will secure the election of Delegates
to the Rep State and National
Convention who will be guided in all
Matters by the wishes of the said party
of the first part and will also secure
the election of member of the State
Senate from the 43 - 44 and 45
Senatorial districts and also secure the
election of members of the House of
Rep
south of the Allegheny and Ohio Rivers
in the County of Allegheny
who will be guided by the wishes
and request of the said party of
the first part during the continuance of
this agreement upon all political matters

the different contractors for the
various positions mentioned shall be
selected by the parties of the second

Facsimile of the famous Quay-Flinn
"Mutual Political and
Business Advantage Agreement."

the withdrawal of Dr. A. J. Barchfeld, and the parties of the second part shall withdraw as a candidate Senator Steel, and the parties of the second part shall secure the election of some party satisfactory to themselves. In the Twenty-second congressional district the candidates for congress shall be selected by the party of the second part. The term of this agreement to be for —— years from the signing thereof, and shall be binding upon all parties when signed by C. L. Magee."

Thus was the city of Pittsburg turned over by the State to an individual to do with as he pleased. Magee's ring was complete. He was the city, Flinn was the councils, the county was theirs, and now they had the State Legislature so far as Pittsburg was concerned. Magee and Flinn were the government and the law. How could they commit a crime? If they wanted something from the city they passed an ordinance granting it, and if some other ordinance was in conflict it was repealed or amended. If the laws in the State stood in the way, so much the worse for the laws of the State; they were amended. If the constitution of the State proved a barrier, as it did to all special legislation, the Legislature enacted a law for cities of the second class (which was Pittsburg alone) and the courts upheld the Legislature. If there were opposition on the side of public opinion, there was a use for that also.

The new charter which David D. Bruce fought through councils in 1886-87 was an example of the way Magee and, after him, Quay and other Pennsylvania bosses employed popular movements. As his machine grew Magee found council committees unwieldy in some respects, and he wanted a change. He took up Bruce's charter, which centered all executive and administrative power and responsibility in the mayor and heads of departments, passed it through the Legislature, but so amended that the heads of departments were not to be appointed by the mayor, but elected by councils. These elections were by expiring councils, so that the department chiefs held over, and with their patronage insured the re-election of the councilmen who elected them. The Magee-Flinn machine, perfect before, was made self-perpetuating. I know of nothing like it in any other city. Tammany in comparison is a plaything, and in the management of a city Croker was a child beside Chris Magee.

The graft of Pittsburg falls conveniently into four classes: franchises, public contracts, vice, and public funds. There was, besides these, a lot of miscellaneous loot—public supplies, public lighting, and the water supply. You hear of second-class fire-engines taken at first-class prices, water rents from the public works kept up because a private concern that supplied the South Side could charge no more than the city, a gas contract to supply the city lightly availed of. But I cannot go into these. Neither can I stop for the details of the system by which public funds were left at no interest with favored depositories from which the city borrowed at a high rate, or the removal of funds to a bank in which the ringsters were shareholders. All these things were managed well within the law, and that was the great principle underlying the Pittsburg plan.

The vice graft, for example, was not blackmail as it is in New York and most other cities. It is a legitimate business, conducted, not by the police, but in an orderly fashion by syndicates, and the chairman of one of the parties at the last election said it was worth $250,000 a year. I saw a man who was laughed at for offering $17,500 for the slot-machine concession; he was told that it was let for much more. "Speak-easies" (unlicensed drinking places) pay so well that when they earn $500 or more in twenty-four hours their proprietors often make a bare living. Disorderly houses are managed by ward syndicates. Permission is had from the syndicate real estate agent, who alone can rent them. The syndicate hires a house from the owners at, say, $35 a month, and he lets it to a woman at from $35 to $50 a week. For furniture the tenant must go to the "official furniture man," who delivers $1000 worth of "fixings" for a note for $3000, on which high interest must be paid. For beer the tenant must go to the "official bottler," and pay $2 for a one-dollar case of beer; for wines and liquors to the "official liquor commissioner," who charges $10 for five dollars' worth; for clothes to the "official wrapper maker." These women may not buy shoes, hats, jewelry, or any other luxury or necessity except from the official concessionaries, and then only at the official, monopoly prices. If the victims have anything left, a police or some other city official is said to call and get it (there are rich ex-police officials in Pittsburg). But this is blackmail and outside the system, which is well understood in the community. Many men, in various walks of life, told me separately the names of the official bottlers, jewelers, and furnishers; they are notorious, but they are safe. They do nothing illegal. Oppressive, wretched, what you please, the Pittsburg system is safe.

That was the keynote of the Flinn-Magee plan, but this vice graft was not their business. They are credited with the suppression of disorder and decent superficial regulations of vice, which is a characteristic of Pittsburg. I know it is said that under the Philadelphia and Pittsburg plans, which are much alike, "all graft and all patronage go across one table," but if any "dirty money" reached the Pittsburg bosses it was, so far as I could prove, in the form of contributions to the party fund, and came from the vice dealers only as it did from other business men.

Magee and Flinn, owners of Pittsburg, made Pittsburg their business, and, monopolists in the technical economic sense of the word, they prepared to exploit it as if it were their private property. For convenience they divided it between them. Magee took the financial and corporate branch, turning the streets to his uses, delivering to himself franchises, and building and running railways. Flinn went in for public contracts for his firm, Booth & Flinn, Ltd., and his branch boomed. Old streets were repaved, new ones laid out; whole districts were improved, parks made, and buildings erected. The improvement of their city went on at a great rate for years, with only one period of cessation, and the period of economy was when Magee was building so many traction lines that Booth & Flinn, Ltd., had all they could do with this work. It was said that no other contractors had an adequate "plant" to supplement properly the work of Booth & Flinn, Ltd. Perhaps that was why this firm had to do such a large proportion of the public work always. Flinn's Director of Public Works was E. M. Bigelow, a cousin of Chris Magee and another nephew of old Squire Steele. Bigelow, called the Extravagant, drew the specifications; he made the awards to the lowest *responsible* bidders, and he inspected and approved the work while in progress and when done.

Flinn had a quarry, the stone of which was specified for public buildings; he obtained the monopoly of a certain kind of asphalt, and that kind was specified. Nor was this all. If the official contractor had done his work well and at reasonable prices the city would not have suffered directly; but his methods were so oppressive upon property holders that they caused a scandal. No action was taken, however, till Oliver McClintock, a merchant, in rare civic wrath, contested the contracts and fought them through the courts. This single citizen's long, brave fight is one of the finest stories in the history of municipal government. The frowns and warnings of cowardly fellow-citizens did not move him, nor the boycott of other business men, the threats of the ring, and the ridicule of ring organs. George W. Guthrie joined him later, and though they fought on undaunted, they were beaten again and again. The Director of Public Works controlled the initiative in court proceedings; he chose the judge who appointed the Viewers, with the result, Mr. McClintock reported, that the Department prepared the Viewers' reports. Knowing no defeat, Mr. McClintock photographed Flinn's pavements at places where they were torn up to show that "large stones, as they were excavated from sewer trenches, brick bats, and the débris of old coal-tar sidewalks were promiscuously dumped in to make foundations, with the result of an uneven settling of the foundation, and the sunken and worn places so conspicuous everywhere in the pavements of the East End." One outside asphalt company tried to break the monopoly, but was easily beaten in 1889, withdrew, and after that one of its officers said, "We all gave Pittsburg a wide berth, recognizing the uselessness of offering competition so long as the door of the Department of Public Works is locked against us, and Booth & Flinn are permitted to carry the key." The monopoly caused not only high prices on short guarantee, but carried with it all the contingent work. Curbing and grading might have been let separately, but they were not. In one contract Mr. McClintock cites, Booth & Flinn bid 50 cents for 44,000 yards of grading.

E. H. Bochman offered a bid of 15 cents for the grading as a separate contract, and his bid was rejected. A property-owner on Shady Lane, who was assessed for curbing at 80 cents a foot, contracted privately at the same time for 800 feet of the same standard curbing, from the same quarry, and set in place in the same manner, at 40 cents a foot!

"During the nine years succeeding the adoption of the charter of 1887," says Mr. Oliver McClintock in a report to the National Municipal League, "one firm [Flinn's] received practically all the asphalt-paving contracts at prices ranging from $1 to $1.80 per square yard higher than the average price paid in neighboring cities. Out of the entire amount of asphalt pavements laid during these nine years, represented by 193 contracts, and costing $3,551,131, only nine street blocks paved in 1896, and costing $33,400, were not laid by this firm."

The building of bridges in this city of bridges, the repairing of pavements, park-making, and real estate deals in anticipation of city improvements were all causes of scandal to some citizens, sources of profit to others who were "let in on the ground floor." There is no space for these here. Another exposure came in 1897 over the contracts for a new Public Safety Building. J. O. Brown was Director of Public Safety. A newspaper, the *Leader*, called attention to a deal for this work, and George W. Guthrie and William B. Rogers, leading members of the Pittsburg bar, who followed up the subject, discovered as queer a set of specifications for the building itself as any city has on record. Favored contractors were named or their wares described all through, and a letter to the architect from J. O. Brown contained specifications for such favoritism, as, for example: "Specify the Westinghouse electric-light plant and engines straight." "Describe the Van Horn Iron Co.'s cells as close as possible." The stone clause was Flinn's, and that is the one that raised the rumpus. Flinn's quarry produced Ligonier block, and Ligonier block was specified. There was a letter from Booth & Flinn, Ltd., telling the architect that the price was to be specified at $31,500. A local contractor offered to provide Tennessee granite set up, a more expensive material, on which the freight is higher, at $19,880; but that did not matter. When another local contracting firm, however, offered to furnish Ligonier block set up at $18,000, a change was necessary, and J. O. Brown directed the architect to "specify that the Ligonier block shall be of a bluish tint rather than a gray variety." Flinn's quarry had the bluish tint, the other people's "the gray variety." It was shown also that Flinn wrote to the architect on June 24, 1895, saying: "I have seen Director Brown and Comptroller Gourley to-day, and they have agreed to let us start on the working plans and get some stone out for the new building. Please arrange that we may get the tracings by Wednesday. . . ." The tracings were furnished him, and thus before the advertisements for bids were out he began preparing the bluish tint stone. The charges were heard by a packed committee of councils, and nothing came of them; and, besides, they were directed against the Director of Public Works, not William Flinn.

The boss was not an official, and not responsible. The only time Flinn was in danger was on a suit that grew out of the conviction of the City Attorney, W. C. Moreland, and L. H. House, his assistant, for the embezzlement of public funds. These officials were found to be short about $300,000. One of them pleaded guilty, and both went to prison without telling where the money went, and that information did not develop till later. J. B. Connelly, of the *Leader*, discovered in the City Attorney's office stubs of checks indicating that some $118,000 of it had gone to Flinn or to Booth & Flinn, Ltd. When Flinn was first asked about it by a reporter he said that the items were correct, that he got them, but that he had explained it all to the Comptroller and had satisfied him. This answer indicated a belief that the money belonged to the city. When he was sued by the city he said that he did not know it was city money. He thought it was personal loans from House. Now House was not a well-to-do man, and his city salary was but $2,500 a year. Moreover, the checks, two of which are reproduced here, are signed by the City Attorney, W. C. Moreland, and are for amounts ranging from five to fifteen thousand dollars. But where was the money? Flinn testified that he had paid it back to House. Then where were the receipts? Flinn said they had been burned in a fire that had occurred in Booth & Flinn's office. The judge found for Flinn, holding that it had not been proven that Flinn knew the checks were for public money, nor that he had not repaid the amount.

As I have said before, however, unlawful acts were exceptional and unnecessary in Pittsburg. Magee did not steal franchises and sell them. His councils gave them to him. He and the busy Flinn took them, built railways, which Magee sold and bought and financed and conducted, like any other man whose successful career is held up as an example for young men. His railways, combined into the Consolidated Traction Company, were capitalized at $30,000,000. The public debt of Pittsburg is about $18,000,000, and the profit on the railway building of Chris Magee would have wiped out the debt. "But you must remember," they say in the Pittsburg banks, "that Magee took risks, and his profits are the just reward of enterprise." This is business. But politically speaking it was an abuse of the powers of a popular ruler for Boss Magee to give to Promoter Magee all the streets he wanted in Pittsburg at his own terms: forever, and nothing to pay. There was scandal in Chicago over the granting of charters for twenty-eight and fifty years. Magee's read: "for 950 years," "for 999 years," "said Charter is to exist a thousand years," "said Charter is to exist perpetually," and the councils gave franchises for the "life of the Charter." There is a legend that Fred Magee, a waggish brother of Chris, put these phrases into these grants for fun, and no doubt the genial Chris saw the fun of it. I asked if the same joker put in the car tax, which is the only compensation the city gets for the use forever of its streets; but it was explained that that was an oversight. The car tax was put upon the old horse-cars, and came down upon the trolley because, having been left unpaid, it was forgotten. This car tax on $30,000,000 of property amounts to less than $15,000 a year, and the companies have until lately been slow about paying it. During the twelve years succeeding 1885 all the traction companies together paid the city $60,000. While the horse vehicles in 1897 paid $47,000, and bicycles $7,000, the Consolidated Traction Company* (C. L. Magee, President) paid $9,600. The speed of bicycles and horse vehicles is limited by law, that of the trolley is unregulated. The only re-

* All the street railways terminating in the city of Pittsburg were in 1901 consolidated into the Pittsburg Railways Company, operating 404 miles of track, under an approximate capitalization of $84,000,000. In their statement, issued July 1, 1902, they report gross earnings for 1901 as $7,181,452.82. Out of this they paid a car tax for 1902 to the city of Pittsburg of $20,099.94. At the ordinary rate of 5 per cent. on gross earnings the tax would have been $354,072.60.

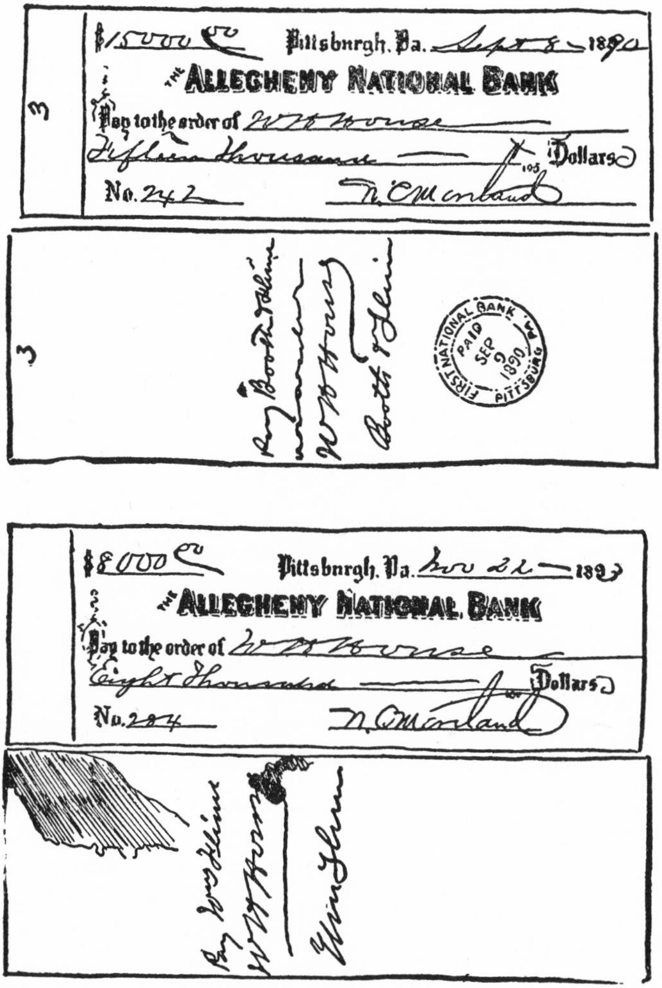

Facsimile of checks showing that public money, embezzled by public officials, went to Boss Flinn, who explained that he did not know the checks were for city money.

quirement of the law upon them is that the traction company shall keep in repair the pavement between and a foot outside of the tracks. This they don't do, and they make the city furnish twenty policemen as guards for crossings of their lines at a cost of $20,000 a year in wages.

Not content with the gift of the streets, the ring made the city work for the railways. The building of bridges is one function of the municipality as a servant of the traction company. Pittsburg is a city of many bridges, and many of them were built for ordinary traffic. When the Magee railways went over them some of them had to be rebuilt. The company asked the city to do it, and despite the protests of citizens and newspapers, the city rebuilt iron bridges in good condition and of recent construction to accommodate the tracks. Once some citizens applied for a franchise to build a connecting line along what is now part of the Bloomfield route, and by way of compensation offered to build a bridge across the Pennsylvania tracks for free city use, they only to have the right to run their cars on it. They did not get their franchise. Not long after Chris Magee (and Flinn) got it, and they got it for nothing; and the city built this bridge, rebuilt three other bridges over the Pennsylvania tracks, and one over the Junction Railroad—five bridges in all, at a cost of $160,000!

Canny Scots as they were, the Pittsburgers submitted to all this for a quarter of a century, and some $34,000 has been subscribed toward the monument to Chris Magee. This sounds like any other well-broken American city; but to the credit of Pittsburg be it said that there never was a time when some few individuals were not fighting the ring. David D. Bruce was standing for good government way back in the 'fifties. Oliver McClintock and George W. Guthrie we have had glimpses of, struggling, like John Hampden, against their tyrants; but always for mere justice and in the courts, and all in vain, till in 1895 their exposures began to bring forth signs of public feeling, and they ventured to appeal to the voters, the sources of the bosses' power. They enlisted the venerable Mr. Bruce and a few other brave men, and together called a mass-meeting. A crowd gathered. There were not many prominent men there, but evidently the people were with them, and they then and there formed the Municipal League, and launched it upon a campaign to beat the ring at the February election, 1896.

A committee of five was put in charge—Bruce, McClintock, George K. Stevenson, Dr. Pollock, and Otto Heeren —who combined with Mr. Guthrie's sterling remnant of the Democratic party on an independent ticket, with Mr. Guthrie at the head for mayor. It was a daring thing to do, and they discovered then what we have discovered in St. Louis and Minneapolis. Mr. Bruce told me that, after their mass-meeting, men who should have come out openly for the movement approached him by stealth and whispered that he could count on them for money if he would keep secret their names. "Outside of those at the meeting," he said, "but one man of all those that subscribed would let his name appear. And men who gave me information to use against the ring spoke themselves for the ring on the platform." Mr. McClintock in a paper read before a committee of the National Municipal League says: "By far the most disheartening discovery, however, was that of the apathetic indifference of many representative citizens—men who from every other point of view are deservedly looked upon as model members of society. We found that prominent merchants and contractors who were 'on the inside,' manufacturers enjoying special municipal privileges, wealthy capitalists, brokers, and others who were holders of the securities of traction and other corporations, had their mouths stopped, their convictions of duty strangled, and their influence before and votes on election day pre-empted against us. In still another direction we found that the financial and political support of the great steam railroads and largest manufacturing corporations, controlling as far as they were able the suffrages of their thousands of employees, were thrown against us, for the simple reason, as was frankly explained by one of them, that it was much easier to deal with a boss in promoting their corporate interests than to deal directly with the people's representatives in the municipal legislature. We even found the directors of many banks in an attitude of cold neutrality, if not of active hostility, toward any movement for municipal reform. As one of them put it, 'if you want to be anybody, or make money in Pittsburg, it is necessary to be in the political swim and on the side of the city ring.' "

This is corruption, but it is called "good business," and it is worse than politics.

It was a quarrel among the grafters of Minneapolis that gave the grand jury a chance there. It was a low row among the grafters of St. Louis that gave Joseph W. Folk his opening. And so in Pittsburg it was in a fight between Quay and Magee that the Municipal League saw its opportunity.

To Quay it was the other way around. The rising of the people of Pittsburg was an opportunity for him. He and Magee had never got along well together, and they were falling out and having their differences adjusted by Flinn and others every few years. The "mutual business advantage" agreement was to have closed one of these rows. The fight of 1895-96 was an especially bitter one, and it did not close with the "harmony" that was patched up. Magee and Flinn and Boss Martin of Philadelphia set out to kill Quay politically, and he, driven thus into one of those "fights for his life" which make his career so interesting, hearing the grumbling in Philadelphia and seeing the revolt of the citizens of Pittsburg, stepped boldly forth upon a platform for reform, especially to stop the "use of money for the corruption of our cities." From Quay this was comical, but the Pittsburgers were too serious to laugh. They were fighting for their life, too, so to speak, and the sight of a boss on their side must have encouraged those business men who "found it easier to deal with a boss than with the people's representatives." However that may be, a majority of the ballots cast in the municipal election of Pittsburg in February, 1896, were against the ring.

This isn't history. According to the records the reform ticket was defeated by about 1000 votes. The returns up to one o'clock on the morning after election showed George W. Guthrie far ahead for mayor; then all returns ceased suddenly, and when the count came in officially, a few days later, the ring had won. But besides the *prima facie* evidence of fraud, the ringsters afterward told in confidence not only that Mr. Guthrie was counted out, but how it was done. Mr. Guthrie's appeal to the courts, however, for a recount was denied. The courts held that the secret ballot law forbade the opening of the ballot boxes.

Thus the ring held Pittsburg—but not the Pittsburgers. They saw Quay in control of the Legislature, Quay the reformer, who would help them. So they drew a charter for Pittsburg which would restore the city to the people. Quay saw the instrument, and he approved it; he promised to have it passed. The League, the Chamber of Commerce, and other representative bodies, all encouraged by the outlook for victory, sent to Harrisburg committees to urge their charter, and their orators poured forth upon the Magee-Flinn ring a flood of, not invective, but facts, specifications of outrage, and the abuse of absolute power. Their charter went booming along through its first and second readings, Quay and the Magee-Flinn crowd fighting inch by inch. All looked well, when suddenly there was silence. Quay was dealing with his enemies, and the charter was his club. He wanted to go back to the Senate, and he went. The Pittsburgers saw him elected, saw him go, but their charter they saw no more. And such is the State of Pennsylvania that this man who did this thing to Pittsburg, and has done the like again and again to all cities and all interests—even politicians—he is the boss of Pennsylvania to-day!

The good men of Pittsburg gave up, and for four years the essential story of the government of the city is a mere thread in the personal history of the quarrels of the bosses in State politics. Magee wanted to go to the United States Senate, and he had with him Boss Martin and John Wanamaker of Philadelphia, as well as his own Flinn. Quay turned on the city bosses, and, undermining their power, soon had Martin beaten in Philadelphia. To overthrow Magee was a harder task, and Quay might never have accomplished it had not Magee's health failed, causing him to be much away. Pittsburg was left to Flinn, and his masterfulness, unmitigated by Magee, made trouble. The crisis came out of a row Flinn had with his Director of Public Works, E. M. Bigelow, a man as dictatorial as

Flinn himself. Bigelow threw open to competition certain contracts. Flinn, in exasperation, had the councils throw out the director and put in his place a man who restored the old specifications.

This enraged Thomas Steele Bigelow, E. M. Bigelow's brother, and another nephew of old Squire Steele. Tom had an old grudge against Magee, dating from the early days of traction deals. He was rich, he knew something of politics, and he believed in the power of money in the game. Going straight to Harrisburg, he took charge of Quay's fight for Senator, spent his own money and won; and he beat Magee, which was his first purpose.

But he was not satisfied yet. The Pittsburgers, aroused to fresh hope by the new fight of the bosses, were encouraged also by the news that the census of 1900 put a second city, Scranton, into "cities of the second class." New laws had to be drawn for both. Pittsburg saw a chance for a good charter. Tom Bigelow saw a chance to finish the Magee-Flinn ring, and he had William B. Rogers, a man whom the city trusted, draw the famous "Ripper Bill"! This was originally a good charter, concentrating power in the mayor, but changes were introduced into it to enable the Governor to remove and appoint mayors, or recorders, as they were to be called, at will until April, 1903, when the first elected recorder was to take office. This was Bigelow's device to rid Pittsburg of the ring office holders. But Magee was not dead yet. He and Flinn saw Governor Stone, and when the Governor ripped out the ring mayor, he appointed as recorder Major A. M. Brown, a lawyer well thought of in Pittsburg.

Major Brown, however, kept all but one of the ring heads of the departments. This disappointed the people; it was a defeat for Bigelow; for the ring it was a triumph.

Without Magee, however, Flinn could not hold his fellows in their joy, and they went to excesses which exasperated Major Brown and gave Bigelow an excuse for urging him to action. Major Brown suddenly removed the heads of the ring and began a thorough reorganization of the government. This reversed emotions, but not for long. The ring leaders saw Governor Stone again, and he ripped out Bigelow's Brown and appointed in his place a ring Brown. Thus the ring was restored to full control under a charter which increased their power.

But the outrageous abuse of the Governor's unusual power over the city incensed the people of Pittsburg. A postscript which Governor Stone added to his announcement of the appointment of the new recorder did not help matters; it was a denial that he had been bribed. The Pittsburgers had not heard of any bribery, but the postscript gave currency to a definite report that the ring—its banks, its corporations, and its bosses—had raised an enormous fund to pay the Governor for his interference in the city, and this pointed the intense feelings of the citizens. They prepared to beat the ring at an election to be held in February, 1902, for Comptroller and half of the councils. A Citizens' party was organized. The campaign was an excited one; both sides did their best, and the vote polled was the largest ever known in Pittsburg. Even the ring made a record. The citizens won, however, and by a majority of 8,000.

This showed the people what they could do when they tried, and they were so elated that they went into the next election and carried the county—the stronghold of the ring. But they now had a party to look out for, and they did not look out for it. They neglected it just as they had the city. Tom Bigelow knew the value of a majority party; he had appreciated the Citizens' from the start. Indeed he may have started it. All the reformers know is that the committee which called the Citizens' Party into existence was made up of twenty-five men—five old Municipal Leaguers, the rest a "miscellaneous lot." They did not bother then about that. They knew Tom Bigelow, but he did not show himself, and the new party went on confidently with its passionate work.

When the time came for the great election, that for recorder this year (1903), the citizens woke up one day and found Tom Bigelow the boss of their party. How he came there they did not exactly know; but there he was in full possession, and there with him was the "miscellaneous lot" on the committee. Moreover, Bigelow was applying with vigor regular machine methods. It was all very astonishing, but very significant. Magee was dead; Flinn's end was in sight; but there was the Boss, the everlasting American Boss, as large as life. The good citizens were shocked; their dilemma was ridiculous, but it was serious too. Helpless, they watched. Bigelow nominated for recorder a man they never would have chosen. Flinn put up a better man, hoping to catch the citizens, and when these said they could see Flinn behind his candidate, he said, "No; I am out of politics. When Magee died I died politically, too." Nobody would believe him. The decent Democrats hoped to retrieve their party and offer a way out, but Bigelow went into their convention with his money and the wretched old organization sold out. The smell of money on the Citizens' side attracted to it the grafters, the rats from Flinn's sinking ship; many of the corporations went over, and pretty soon it was understood that the railroads had come to a settlement among themselves and with the new boss, on the basis of an agreement said to contain five specifications of grants from the city. The temptation to vote for Flinn's man was strong, but the old reformers seemed to feel that the only thing to do was to finish Flinn now and take care of Tom Bigelow later. This view prevailed and Tom Bigelow won. This is the way the best men in Pittsburg put it: "We have smashed a ring and we have wound another around us. Now we have got to smash that."

There is the spirit of this city as I understand it. Craven as it was for years, corrupted high and low, Pittsburg did rise; it shook off the superstition of partisanship in municipal politics; beaten, it rose again; and now, when it might have boasted of a triumph, it saw straight: a defeat. The old fighters, undeceived and undeceiving, humiliated but undaunted, said simply: "All we have got to do is to begin all over again." Meanwhile, however, Pittsburg has developed some young men, and with an inheritance of this same spirit, they are going to try out in their own way. The older men undertook to save the city with a majority party and they lost the party. The younger men have formed a Voters' Civic League, which proposes to swing from one party to another that minority of disinterested citizens which is always willing to be led, and thus raise the standard of candidates and improve the character of regular party government. Tom Bigelow intended to capture the old Flinn organization, combine it with his Citizens' party, and rule as Magee did with one party, a union of all parties. If he should do this, the young reformers would have no two parties to choose between; but there stand the old fighters ready to rebuild a Citizens' party under that or any other name. Whatever course is taken, however, something will be done in Pittsburg, or tried, at least, for good government, and after the cowardice and corruption shamelessly displayed in other cities, the effort of Pittsburg, pitiful as it is, is a spectacle good for American self-respect, and its sturdiness is a promise for poor old Pennsylvania.

Philadelphia: Corrupt and Contented

(*July, 1903*)

Other American cities, no matter how bad their own condition may be, all point with scorn to Philadelphia as worse—"the worst-governed city in the country." St Louis, Minneapolis, Pittsburg submit with some patience to the jibes of any other community; the most friendly suggestion from Philadelphia is rejected with contempt. The Philadelphians are "supine," "asleep"; hopelessly ring-ruled, they are "complacent." "Politically benighted," Philadelphia is supposed to have no light to throw upon a state of things that is almost universal.

This is not fair. Philadelphia is, indeed, corrupt; but it is not without significance. Every city and town in the country can learn something from the typical political experience of this great representative city. New York is excused for many of its ills because it is the metropolis, Chicago because of its forced development; Philadelphia is our "third largest" city and its growth has been gradual and natural. Immigration has been blamed for our municipal conditions; Philadelphia, with 47 per cent. of its population native-born of native-born parents, is the most American of our greater cities. It is "good," too, and intelligent. I don't know just how to measure the intelligence of a community, but a Pennsylvania college professor who declared to me his belief in education for the masses as a way out of political corruption, himself justified the "rake-off" of preferred contractors on public works on the ground of a "fair business profit." Another plea we have made is that we are too busy to attend to public business, and we have promised, when we come to wealth and leisure, to do better. Philadelphia has long enjoyed great and widely distributed prosperity; it is the city of homes; there is a dwelling house for every five persons,—men, women, and children,—of the population; and the people give one a sense of more leisure and repose than any community I ever dwelt in. Some Philadelphians account for their political state on the ground of their ease and comfort. There is another class of optimists whose hope is in an "aristocracy" that is to come by and by; Philadelphia is surer that it has a "real aristocracy" than any other place in the world, but its aristocrats, with few exceptions, are in the ring, with it, or of no political use. Then we hear that we are a young people and that when we are older and "have traditions," like some of the old countries, we also will be honest. Philadelphia is one of the oldest of our cities and treasures for us scenes and relics of some of the noblest traditions of "our fair land."

Yet I was told how once, "for a joke," a party of boodlers counted out the "divvy" of their graft in unison with the ancient chime of Independence Hall.

Philadelphia is representative. This very "joke," told, as it was, with a laugh, is typical. All our municipal governments are more or less bad, and all our people are optimists. Philadelphia is simply the most corrupt and the most contented. Minneapolis has cleaned up, Pittsburg has tried to, New York fights every other election, Chicago fights all the time. Even St. Louis has begun to stir (since the elections are over), and at the worst was only shameless. Philadelphia is proud; good people there defend corruption and boast of their machine. My college professor, with his philosophic view of "rake-offs," is one Philadelphia type. Another is the man, who, driven to bay with his local pride, says: "At least you must admit that our machine is the best you have ever seen."

Disgraceful? Other cities say so. But I say that if Philadelphia is a disgrace, it is a disgrace not to itself alone, nor to Pennsylvania, but to the United States and to American character. For this great city, so highly representative in other respects, is not behind in political experience, but ahead, with New York. Philadelphia is a city that has had its reforms. Having passed through all the typical stages of corruption, Philadelphia reached the period of miscellaneous loot with a boss for chief thief, under James McManes and the Gas Ring 'way back in the late sixties and seventies. This is the Tweed stage of corruption from which St. Louis, for example, is just emerging. Philadelphia, in two inspiring popular revolts, attacked the Gas Ring, broke it, and in 1885 achieved that dream of American cities—a good charter. The present condition of Philadelphia, therefore, is not that which precedes, but that which follows reform, and in this distinction lies its startling general significance. What has happened since the Bullitt Law or charter went into effect in Philadelphia may happen in any American city "after reform is over."

For reform with us is usually revolt, not government, and is soon over. Our people do not seek, they avoid self-rule, and "reforms" are spasmodic efforts to punish bad rulers and get somebody that will give us good government or something that will make it. A self-acting form of government is an ancient superstition. We are an inventive people, and we all think that we shall devise some day a legal machine that will turn out good government automatically. The Philadelphians have treasured this belief longer than the rest of us and have tried it more often. Throughout their history they have sought this wonderful charter and they thought they had it when they got the Bullitt Law, which concentrates in the mayor ample power, executive and political, and complete responsibility. Moreover, it calls for very little thought and action on the part of the people. All they expected to have to do when the Bullitt Law went into effect was to elect as mayor a good business man, who, with his probity and common sense, would give them that good business administration which is the ideal of many reformers.

The Bullitt Law went into effect in 1887. A committee of twelve—four men from the Union League, four from business organizations, and four from the bosses—picked out the first man to run under it on the Republican ticket, Edwin H. Fitler, an able, upright business man, and he was elected. Strange to say, his administration was satisfactory to the citizens, who speak well of it to this day, and to the politicians also; Boss McManes (the ring was broken, not the boss) took to the next national convention from Philadelphia a delegation solid for Fitler for President of the United States. It was a farce, but it pleased Mr. Fitler, so Matthew S. Quay, the State boss, let him have a complimentary vote on the first ballot. The politicians "fooled" Mr. Fitler, and they "fooled" also the next business mayor, Edwin S. Stuart, likewise a most estimable gentleman. Under these two administrations the foundation was laid for the present government of Philadelphia, the corruption to which Philadelphians seemed so reconciled, and the machine which is "at least the best you have ever seen."

The Philadelphia machine isn't the best. It isn't sound, and I doubt if it would stand in New York or Chicago. The enduring strength of the typical American political machine is that it is a natural growth—a sucker, but deep-rooted in the people. The New Yorkers vote for Tammany Hall. The Philadelphians do not vote; they are disfranchised, and their disfranchisement is one anchor of the foundation of the Philadelphia organization.

This is no figure of speech. The honest citizens of Philadelphia have no more rights at the polls than the negroes down South. Nor do they fight very hard for this basic privilege. You can arouse their Republican ire by talking about the black Republican votes lost in the Southern States by white Democratic intimidation, but if you remind the average Philadelphian that he is in the same position, he will look startled, then say, "That's so, that's literally true, only I never thought of it in just that way." And it is literally true.

The machine controls the whole process of voting, and practices fraud at every stage. The assessor's list is the voting list, and the assessor is the machine's man. "The assessor of a division kept a disorderly house; he padded his lists with fraudulent names registered from his house; two of these names were used by election officers. . . . The constable of the division kept a disreputable house; a policeman was assessed as living there. . . . The election was held in the disorderly house maintained by the assessor. . . . The man named as judge had a criminal charge for a life offense pending against him. . . . Two hundred and fifty-two votes were returned in a division that had less than one hundred legal votes within its boundaries." These extracts from a report of the Municipal League suggest the election methods. The assessor pads the list with the names of dead dogs, children, and non-existent persons. One newspaper printed the picture of a dog, another that of a little four-year-old negro boy, down on such a list. A ring orator in a speech resenting sneers at his ward as "low down" reminded his hearers that that was the ward of Independence Hall, and naming over signers of the Declaration of Independence, he closed his highest flight of eloquence with the statement that "these men, the fathers of American liberty, voted down here once. And," he added, with a catching grin, "they vote here yet." Rudolph Blankenburg, a persistent fighter for the right and the use of the right to vote (and, by the way, an immigrant), sent out just before one election a registered letter to each voter on the rolls of a certain selected division. Sixty-three per cent. were returned marked "not at," "removed," "deceased," etc. From one four-story house where forty-four voters were addressed, eighteen letters came back undelivered; from another of forty-eight voters, came back forty-one letters; from another sixty-one out of sixty-two; from another, forty-four out of forty-seven. Six houses in one divsion were assessed at one hundred and seventy-two voters, more than the votes cast in the previous election in any one of two hundred entire divisions.

The repeating is done boldly, for the machine controls the election officers, often choosing them from among the fraudulent names; and when no one appears to serve, assigning the heeler ready for the expected vacancy. The police are forbidden by law to stand within thirty feet of the polls, but they are at the box and they are there to see that the machine's orders are obeyed and that repeaters whom they help to furnish are permitted to vote without "intimidation" on the names they, the police, have supplied. The editor of an anti-machine paper who was looking about for himself once told me that a ward leader who knew him well asked him into a polling place. "I'll show you how it's done," he said, and he had the repeaters go round and round voting again and again on the names handed them on slips. "But," as the editor said, "that isn't the way it's done." The repeaters go from one polling place to another, voting on slips, and on their return rounds change coats, hats, etc. The business proceeds with very few hitches; there is more jesting than fighting. Violence in the past has had its effect; and is not often necessary nowadays, but if it is needed the police are there to apply it. Several citizens told me that they had seen the police help to beat citizens or elections officers who were trying to do their duty, then arrest the victim; and Mr. Clinton Rogers Woodruff, the executive counsel of the Municipal League, has published a booklet of such cases. But an official statement of the case is at hand in an announcement by John Weaver, the new machine mayor of Philadelphia, that he is going to keep the police out of politics and away from the polls. "I shall see," he added, "that every voter enjoys the full right of suffrage and that ballots may be placed in the ballot box without fear of intimidation."

But many Philadelphians do not try to vote. They leave everything to the machine, and the machine casts their ballots for them. It is estimated that 150,000 voters did not go to the polls at the last election. Yet the machine rolled up a majority of 130,000 for Weaver, with a fraudulent vote estimated all the way from forty to eighty thousand, and this in a campaign so machine-made that it was called "no contest." Francis Fisher Kane, the Democrat, got 32,000 votes out of some 204,000. "What is the use of voting?" these stay-at-homes ask. A friend of mine told me he was on the lists in the three wards in which he had successively dwelt. He votes personally in none, but the leader of his present ward tells him how he has been voted. Mr. J. C. Reynolds, the proprietor of the St. James Hotel, went to the polls at eleven o'clock last election day, only to be told that he had been voted. He asked how many others from his house had voted. An election officer took up a list, checked off twelve names, two down twice, and handed it to him. When Mr. Reynolds got home he learned that one of these had voted, the others had been voted. Another man said he rarely attempted to vote, but when he did, the officers let him, even though his name had already been voted on; and then the negro repeaters would ask if his "brother was coming 'round to-day." They were going to vote him, as they vote all good-natured citizens who stay away. "When this kind of man turns out," said a leader to me, "we simply have two repeaters extra—one to balance him and one more to the good." If necessary, after all this, the machine counts the vote "right," and there is little use appealing to the courts, since they have held, except in one case, that the ballot box is secret and cannot be opened. The only legal remedy lies in the purging of the assessor's lists, and when the Municipal League had this done in 1899, they reported that there was "wholesale voting on the very names stricken off."

Deprived of self-government, the Philadelphians haven't even self-governing machine government. They have their own boss, but he and his machine are subject to the State ring, and take their orders from the State boss, Matthew S. Quay, who is the proprietor of Pennsylvania and the real ruler of Philadelphia, just as William Penn, the Great Proprietor, was. Philadelphians, especially the local bosses, dislike this description of their government, and they point for refutation to their charter. But this very Bullitt Law was passed by Quay, and he put it through the Legislature, not for reform reasons, but at the instance of David H. Lane, his Philadelphia lieutenant, as a check upon the power of Boss McManes. Later, when McManes proved hopelessly insubordinate, Quay decided to have done with him forever. He chose David Martin for boss, and from his seat in the United States Senate, Penn's successor raised up his man and set him over the people. Croker, who rose by his own strength to the head of Tammany Hall, has tried twice to appoint a successor; no one else could, and he failed. The boss of Tammany Hall is a growth. So Croker has attempted to appoint district leaders and failed; a Tammany district leader is a growth. Boss Martin, picked up and set down from above, was accepted by Philadelphia and the Philadelphia machine, and he removed old ward leaders and appointed new ones. Some leaders in Philadelphia own their wards, of course, but Martin and, after him,

Durham have sent men into a ward to lead it, and they have led it.

The Philadelphia organization is upside down. It has its root in the air, or, rather, like the banyan tree, it sends its roots from the center out both up and down and all around, and there lies its peculiar strength. For when I said it was dependent and not sound, I did not mean that it was weak. It is dependent as a municipal machine, but the organization that rules Philadelphia is, as we have seen, not a mere municipal machine, but a city, State, and national organization. The people of Philadelphia are Republicans in a Republican city in a Republican State in a Republican nation, and they are bound ring on ring on ring. The President of the United States and his patronage; the National Cabinet and their patronage; the Congress and the patronage of the Senators and the Congressmen from Pennsylvania; the Governor of the State and the State Legislature with their powers and patronage; and all that the mayor and city councils have of power and patronage—all these bear down upon Philadelphia to keep it in the control of Quay's boss and his little ring. This is the ideal of party organization, and, possibly, is the end toward which our democratic republic is tending. If it is, the end is absolutism. Nothing but a revolution could overthrow this oligarchy, and there is its danger. With no outlet at the polls for public feeling, the machine cannot be taught anything it does not know except at the cost of annihilation.

But the Philadelphia machine-leaders know their business. As I said in "Tweed Days in St. Louis," the politicians will learn, if the people won't, from exposure and reform. The Pennsylvania bosses learned the "uses of reform"; we have seen Quay applying it to discipline

McManes, and he since has turned reformer himself, to punish local bosses. The bosses have learned also the danger of combination between citizens and the Democrats. To prevent this, Quay and his friends have spread sedulously the doctrine of "reform within the party," and, from the Committee of One Hundred on, the reformers have stuck pretty faithfully to this principle. But lest the citizens should commit such a sin against their party, Martin formed a permanent combination of the Democratic with the Republican organization, using to that end a goodly share of the Federal and county patronage. Thus the people of Philadelphia were "fixed" so that they couldn't vote if they wanted to, and if they should want to, they couldn't vote for a Democrat, except of Republican or independent choosing. In other words, having taken away their ballot, the bosses took away also the choice of parties.

But the greatest lesson learned and applied was that of conciliation and "good government." The people must not want to vote or rebel against the ring. This ring, like any other, was formed for the exploitation of the city for private profit, and the cementing force is the "cohesive power of public plunder." But McManes and Tweed had proved that miscellaneous larceny was dangerous, and why should a lot of cheap politicians get so much and the people nothing at all? The people had been taught to expect but little from their rulers: good water, good light, clean streets well paved, fair transportation, the decent repression of vice, public order and public safety, and no scandalous or open corruption, would more than satisfy them. It would be good business and good politics to give them these things. Like Chris Magee, who studied out the problem with him, Martin took away from the rank and file of the party and from the ward leaders and office holders the privilege of theft, and he formed companies and groups to handle the legitimate public business of the city. It was all graft, but it was to be all lawful, and, in the main, it was. Public franchises, public works, and public contracts were the principal branches of the business, and Martin adopted the dual boss idea, which we have seen worked out by Magee and Flinn in Pittsburg. In Philadelphia it was Martin and Porter, and just as Flinn had a firm, Booth & Flinn, Ltd., so Porter was Filbert and Porter.

Filbert and Porter got all the public contracts they could handle, and the rest went to other contractors friendly to them and to the ring. Sometimes the preferred contractor was the lowest bidder, but he did not have to be. The law allowed awards to be the "lowest and best," and the courts held that this gave the officials discretion. But since public criticism was to be considered, the ring, to keep up appearances, resorted to many tricks. One was to have fake bids made above the favorite. Another was to have the favorite bid high, but set an impossible time limit; the department of the city councils could extend the time afterwards. Still another was to arrange for specifications which would make outsiders bid high, then either openly alter the plans or let the ring firm perform work not up to requirements.

Many of Martin's deals and jobs were scandals, but they were safe; they were in the direction of public service; and the great mass of the business was done quietly. Moreover, the public was getting something for its money,—not full value, but a good percentage. In other words, there was a limit to the "rake-off," and some insiders have told me that it had been laid down as a principle with the ring that the people should have in value (that is, in work or benefit, including a fair profit) ninety-five cents out of every dollar. In some of the deals I have investigated, the "rake-off" over and above profit was as high as twenty-five per cent. Still, even at this, there was "a limit," and the public was getting, as one of the leaders told me, "a run for its money." Cynical as it all sounds, this view is taken by many Philadelphians almost if not quite as intelligent as my college professor.

But there was another element in the policy of conciliation which is a potent factor in the contentment of Philadelphia, and I regard it as the key to that "apathy" which has made the community notorious. We have seen how Quay had with him the Federal resources and those of the State, and the State ring, and we have seen how Martin, having the city, mayor, and councils, won over the Democratic city leaders. Here they had under pay in office at least 15,000 men and women. But each of these 15,000 persons was selected for office because he could deliver votes, either by organizations, by parties, or by families. These must represent pretty near a majority of the city's voters. But this is by no means the end of the ring's reach. In the State ring are the great corporations, the Standard Oil Company, Cramp's Shipyard, and the steel companies, with the Pennsylvania Railroad at their head, and all the local transportation and other public utility companies following after. They get franchises, privileges, exemptions, etc.; they have helped finance Quay through deals: the Pennsylvania paid Martin, Quay said once, a large yearly salary; the Cramps get contracts to build United States ships, and for years have been begging for a subsidy on home-made ships. The officers, directors, and stockholders of these companies, with their friends, their bankers, and their employees, are of the organization. Better still, one of the local bosses of Philadelphia told me he could always give a worker a job with these companies, just as he could in a city department, or in the mint, or post-office. Then there are the bankers who enjoy, or may some day enjoy, public deposits; those that profit on loans to finance political financial deals; the promoting capitalists who share with the bosses on franchises; and the brokers who deal in ring securities and speculation on ring tips. Through the exchange the ring financiers reach the investing public, which is a large and influential body. The traction companies, which bought their way from beginning to end by corruption, which have always been in the ring, and whose financiers have usually shared in other big ring deals, adopted early the policy of bribing the people with "small blocks of stock." Dr. Frederick Speirs, in his "The Street Railway System of Philadelphia," came upon transactions which "indicate clearly that it is the policy of the Union Company to get the securities into the hands of a large number of small holders, the plain inference being that a wide distribution of securities will fortify the company against possible attacks by the public." In 1895 he found a director saying: "Our critics have engaged the Academy of Music, and are to call an assemblage of people opposed to the street railways as now managed. It would take eight Academies of Music to hold the stockholders of the Union Traction Company."

But we are not yet through. Quay has made a specialty all his life of reformers, and he and his local bosses have won over so many that the list of former reformers is very, very long. Martin drove down his roots through race and religion, too. Philadelphia was one of the hot-beds of "knownothingism." Martin recognized the Catholic, and the Irish-Irish, and so drew off into the Republican party the great natural supply of the Democrats; and his successors have given high places to representative Jews. "Surely this isn't corruption!" No, and neither is that corruption which makes the heads of great educational and charity institutions "go along," as they say in Pennsylvania, in order to get appropriations for their institutions from the State and land from the city. They know what is going on, but they do not join reform movements. The provost of the University of Pennsylvania declined to join in a revolt because, he said, it might impair his usefulness to the University. And so it is with others, and with clergymen who have favorite charities; with Sabbath associations and City Beautiful clubs; with lawyers who want briefs; with real estate dealers who like to know in advance about public improvements, and real estate owners who appreciate light assessments; with shopkeepers who don't want to be bothered with strict inspections.

If there is no other hold for the ring on a man there always is the protective tariff. "I don't care," said a manufacturer. "What if they do plunder and rob us, it can't hurt me unless they raise the tax rates, and even that won't ruin me. Our party keeps up the tariff. If they should reduce that, my business would be ruined."

Such, then, are the ramifications of this machine, such is its strength. No wonder Martin could break his own rules, as he did, and commit excesses. Philadelphia is not merely corrupt, it is corrupted. Martin's doom was proclaimed not in Philadelphia, but in the United States Senate, and his offense was none of this business of his, but his failure to nominate as successor to Mayor Stuart the man, Boise Penrose, whom Matt Quay chose for that place. Martin had consented, but at the last moment he ordered the nomination of Charles F. Warwick instead. The day that happened Mr. Quay arose on the floor of the Senate and, in a speech so irrelevant to the measure under consideration that nobody out of Pennsylvania understood it, said that there was in his town a man who had given as his reason for not doing what he had promised to do, the excuse that he was "under a heavy salary from a great corporation (the Pennsylvania Railroad) and was compelled to do what the corporation wished him to do. And," added Senator Quay, "men in such a position with high power for good or evil ought . . . to go about . . . with the dollar mark of the corporation on their foreheads." Quay named as the new boss Israel W. Durham, a ward leader under Martin.

Martin having the city through Mayor Warwick fought Quay in the State, with Chris Magee for an ally, but Quay beat them both there, and then prepared to beat them in their own cities. His cry was Reform, and he soon had the people shouting for it.

Quay responded with a Legislative committee to investigate abuses in the cities, but this so-called "Lexow" was called off before it amounted to much more than a momentary embarrassment to Martin. Martin's friends, on the other hand, caught Quay and nearly sent him to prison. The People's Bank, James McManes, president, failed. The cashier, John S. Hopkins, had been speculating and letting Quay and other politicians have bank funds without collateral for stock gambling. In return Quay and the State Treasurer left heavy State deposits with the bank. Hopkins lost his nerve and shot himself. McManes happened to call in friends of Martin to advise him, and these suggested a Martin man for receiver. They found among the items money lent to Quay without security, except the State funds, and telegrams asking Hopkins to buy "1000 Met" (Metropolitan) and promising in return to "shake the plum tree." Quay, his son, Richard R., and Benjamin J. Haywood, the State Treasurer, were indicted for conspiracy, and every effort was made to have the trial precede the next election for the Legislature which was to elect a successor to Quay in the United States Senate; but Quay got stays and postponements in the hopes that a more friendly District Attorney could be put in that office. Martin secured the election of Peter F. Rothermel, who was eager to try the case, and Quay had to depend on other resources. The trial came in due course, and failed; Judge Biddle ruled out the essential evidence on the ground that it was excluded by the statute of limitation. Rothermel went on with the trial, but it was hopeless; Quay was acquitted and the other cases were abandoned.

Popular feeling was excited by this exposure of Quay, but there was no action till the factional fighting suggested a use for it. Quay had refused the second United States Senatorship to John Wanamaker, and Wanamaker led through the State and in Philadelphia a fight against the boss, which has never ceased. It took the form of a reform campaign, and Quay's methods were made plain, but the boss beat Wanamaker at every point, had Penrose made Senator, and through Penrose and Durham was gradually getting possession of Philadelphia. The final triumph came with the election of Samuel H. Ashbridge as mayor.

"Stars-and-Stripes Sam," as Ashbridge is sometimes called, was a speech-maker and a "joiner." That is to say, he made a practice of going to lodges, associations, brotherhoods, Sunday-schools, and all sorts of public and private meetings, joining some, but making at all speeches patriotic and sentimental. He was very popular. Under the Bullitt Law, as I have said, all that is necessary to a good administration and complete, though temporary reform, is a good mayor. The politicians feel that they must nominate a man in whom the people as well as themselves have faith. They had had faith in Warwick, both the ring and the people, and Warwick had found it impossible to satisfy two such masters. Now they put their faith in Ashbridge, and so did Durham, and so did Martin. All interests accepted him, therefore, and all watched him with hope and more or less assurance; none more than the good people. And, indeed, no man could have promised more or better public service than Ashbridge. The result, however, was distracting.

Mr. Ashbridge "threw down" Martin, and he recognized Quay's man, "Is" Durham, as the political boss. Durham is a high type of boss, candid, but of few words; generous, but businesslike; complete master of himself, and a genius at organization. For Pennsylvania politics he is a conservative leader, and there would have been no excesses under him, as there have been few "rows." But Mr. Durham has not been the master of the Philadelphia situation. He bowed to Quay, and he could not hold Ashbridge. Philadelphians say that if it should come to a fight, Durham could beat Quay in Philadelphia, but it doesn't come to a fight. Another thing Philadelphians say is that he "keeps his word," yet he broke it (with notice) when Quay asked him to stand for Pennypacker for Governor. As I said before, however, Philadelphia is so constituted that it apparently cannot have self-government, not even its own boss, so that the allegiance paid to Quay is comprehensible. But the submission of the boss to the mayor was extraordinary, and it seemed to some sagacious politicians dangerous.

For Mr. Ashbridge broke through all the principles of moderate grafting developed by Martin. Durham formed his ring—taking in James P. McNichol as co-ruler and preferred contractor; John M. Mack as promoter and financier; and he widened the inside circle to include more individuals. But while he was more liberal toward his leaders, and not inclined "to grab off everything for himself," as one leader told me, he maintained the principle of concentration and strict control as good politics and good business. So, too, he adopted Martin's programme of public improvements, the filtration, boulevards, etc., and he added to it. When Ashbridge was well settled in office, these schemes were all started, and the mayor pushed them with a will. According to the "Philadelphia Plan," the mayor should not be in the ring. He should be an ambitious man, and his reward promotion, not riches. If he is "out for the stuff," he is likely to be hurried by the fretful thought that his term is limited to four years, and since he cannot succeed himself as mayor, his interest in the future of the machine is less than that of a boss, who goes on forever.

When he was nominated, Ashbridge had debts of record amounting to some $40,000. Before he was elected these were satisfied. Soon after he took office he declared himself to former Postmaster Thomas L. Hicks. Here is Mr. Hicks's account of the incident:

"At one of the early interviews I had with the mayor in his office, he said to me: 'Tom, I have been elected mayor of Philadelphia. I have four years to serve. I have no further ambitions. I want no other office when I am out of this one, and I shall get out of this office all there is in it for Samuel H. Ashbridge.'

"I remarked that this was a very foolish thing to say. 'Think how that could be construed,' I said.

" 'I don't care anything about that,' he declared. 'I mean to get out of this office everything there is in it for Samuel H. Ashbridge.' "

When he retired from office last April, he became the president of a bank, and was reputed to be rich. Here is the summary published by the Municipal League at the close of his labors:

"The four years of the Ashbridge administration have passed into history, leaving behind them a scar on the fame and reputation of our city which will be a long time healing. Never before, and let us hope never again, will there be such brazen defiance of public opinion, such flagrant disregard of public interest, such abuse of powers and responsibilities for private ends. These are not generalizations, but each statement can be abundantly proved by numerous instances."

These "numerous instances" are notorious in Philadelphia; some of them were reported all over the country. One of them was the attempted intimidation of John Wanamaker. Thomas B. Wanamaker, John Wanamaker's son, bought the *North American,* a newspaper which had been, and still is, exposing the abuses and corruption of the political ring. Abraham L. English, Mr. Ashbridge's Director of the Department of Public Safety, called on Mr. John Wanamaker, said he had been having him watched, and was finally in a position to demand that the newspaper stop the attacks. The merchant exposed the whole thing, and a committee appointed to investigate reported that: "Mr. English has practically admitted that he attempted to intimidate a reputable citizen and unlawfully threatened him in an effort to silence criticism of a public newspaper; that from the mayor's refusal to order an investigation of the conduct of Mr. English on the request of a town meeting of representative citizens, the community is justified in regarding him as aiding and abetting Mr. English in the corrupt act committed, and that the mayor is therefore to be equally censured by the community."

The other "instances of brazen abuse of power" were the increase of protected vice—the importation from New York of the "white slavery system of prostitution," the growth of "speak-easies," and the spread of gambling and of policy-playing until it took in the school children. This last the *North American* exposed, but in vain till it named police officers who had refused when asked to interfere. Then a judge summoned the editors and reporters of the paper, the mayor, Director English, school children, and police officers to appear before him. The mayor's personal attorney spoke for the police during the inquiry, and it looked black for the newspaper till the children began to tell their stories. When the hearing was over the judge said:

"The evidence shows conclusively that our public school system in this city is in danger of being corrupted at its fountain; that in one of the schools over a hundred and fifty children were buyers of policy, as were also a large number of scholars in other schools. It was first discovered about eighteen months ago, and for about one year has been in full operation." The police officers were not punished, however.

That corruption had reached the public schools and was

spreading rapidly through the system, was discovered by the exposure and conviction of three school directors of the twenty-eighth ward. It was known before that teachers and principals, like any other office holders, had to have a "pull" and pay assessments for election expenses. "Voluntary contributions" was the term used, but over the notices in blue pencil was written "2 per cent.," and teachers who asked directors and ward bosses what to do, were advised that they would "better pay." Those that sent less than the amount suggested, got receipts: "Check received; shall we hold for balance or enter on account?" But the exposure in the twenty-eighth ward brought it home to the parents of the children that the teachers were not chosen for fitness, but for political reasons, and that the political reasons had become cash.

Miss Rena A. Haydock testified as follows: "I went to see Mr. Travis, who was a friend of mine, in reference to getting a teacher's certificate. He advised me to see all of the directors, especially Mr. Brown. They told me that it would be necessary for me to pay $120 to get the place. They told me of one girl who had offered $250, and her application had been rejected. That was before they broached the subject of money to me. I said that I didn't have $120 to pay, and they replied that it was customary for teachers to pay $40 a month out of their first three months' salary. The salary was $47. They told me they didn't want the money for themselves, but that it was necessary to buy the other faction. Finally I agreed to the proposition, and they told me that I must be careful not to mention it to anybody or it would injure my reputation. I went with my brother to pay the money to Mr. Johnson. He held out a hat, and when my brother handed the money to him he took it behind the hat."

The regular business of the ring was like that of Pittsburg, but more extensive. I have space only for one incident of one phase of it: Widener and Elkins, the national franchise buyers, are Philadelphians, and they were in the old Martin ring. They had combined all the street railways of the city before 1900, and they were withdrawing from politics, with their traction system. But the Pennsylvania rings will not let corporations that have risen in corruption reform and retire, and, besides, it was charged that in the Martin-Quay fight, the street railways had put up money to beat Quay for the United States Senate. At any rate, plans were laid to "mace" the street railways.

"Macing" is a form of high blackmail. When they have sold out all they have, the politicians form a competing company and compel the old concern to buy out or sell out. While Widener and Elkins were at sea, bound for Europe, in 1901, the Philadelphia ring went to the Legislature and had introduced there two bills, granting a charter to practically all the streets and alleys not covered by tracks in Philadelphia, and to run short stretches of the old companies' tracks to make connections. Clinton Rogers Woodruff, who was an Assemblyman, has told the story. Without notice the bills were introduced at 3 P.M. on Monday, May 29; they were reported from committee in five minutes; by 8.50 P.M. they were printed and on the members' desk, and by 9 P.M. were passed on first reading. The bills passed second reading the next day, Memorial Day, and on the third day were passed from the Senate to the House, where they were "jammed through" with similar haste and worse trickery. In six legislative days the measures were before Governor Stone, who signed them June 7, at midnight, in the presence of

Quay, Penrose, Congressman Foerderer, Mayor Ashbridge's banker, James P. McNichol, John M. Mack and other capitalists and politicians. Under the law, one hundred charters were applied for the next morning—thirteen for Philadelphia. The charters were granted on June 5, and that same day a special meeting of the Philadelphia Select Council was called for Monday. There the citizens of Philadelphia met the oncoming charters, but their hearing was brief. The charters went through without a hitch, and were sent to Mayor Ashbridge on June 13.

The mayor's secretary stated authoritatively in the morning that the mayor would not sign that day. But he did. An unexpected incident forced his hand. John Wanamaker sent him an offer of $2,500,000 for the franchises about to be given away. Ashbridge threw the letter into the street unread. Mr. Wanamaker had deposited $250,000 as a guarantee of good faith and his action was becoming known. The ordinances were signed by midnight, and the city lost at least two and one-half millions of dollars; but the ring made it and much more. When Mr. Wanamaker's letter was published, Congressman Foerderer, an incorporator of the company, answered for the machine. He said the offer was an advertisement; that it was late, and that they were sorry they hadn't had a chance to "call the bluff." Mr. Wanamaker responded with a renewal of the offer of $2,500,000 to the city, and, he said, "I will add $500,000 as a bonus to yourself and your associates personally for the conveyance of the grants and corporate privileges you now possess." That ended the controversy.

But the deal went on. Two more bills, called "Trolley Chasers," were put through, to finish off the legislation, too hurriedly done to be perfect. One was to give the company the right to build either elevated or underground, or both; the second to forbid all further such grants without a hearing before a board consisting of the Governor, the Secretary of the Commonwealth, and the Attorney-General. With all these franchises and exclusive privileges, the new company made the old one lease their plant in operation to the company which had nothing but "rights," or, in Pennsylvania slang, a "good, husky mace."

Ashbridgeism put Philadelphia and the Philadelphia machine to a test which candid ring leaders did not think it would stand. What did the Philadelphians do? Nothing. They have their reformers: they have men like Francis B. Reeves, who fought with every straight reform movement from the days of the Committee of One Hundred; they have men like Rudolph Blankenburg, who have fought with every reform that promised any kind of relief; there are the Municipal League, with an organization by wards, the Citizens' Municipal League, the Allied Reform League, and the Law and Order Society; there are young men and veterans; there are disappointed politicians and ambitious men who are not advanced fast enough by the machine. There is discontent in a good many hearts, and some men are ashamed. But "the people" won't follow. One would think the Philadelphians would follow any leader; what should they care whether he is pure white or only gray? But they do care. "The people" seem to prefer to be ruled by a known thief than an ambitious reformer. They will make you convict their Tweeds, McManeses, Butlers, and Shepherds, and even then they may forgive them and talk of monuments to their precious memory, but they take delight in the defeat of John

Wanamaker because they suspect that he is a hypocrite and wants to go to the United States Senate.

All the stout-hearted reformers had made a campaign to re-elect Rothermel, the District Attorney who had dared to try Quay. Surely there was an official to support! But no, Quay was against him. The reformers used money, some $250,000, I believe,—fighting the devil with fire,—but the machine used more money, $700,000, from the teachers, "speak-easies," office holders, bankers, and corporations. The machine handled the ballots. Rothermel was beaten by John Weaver. There have been other campaigns, before and since, led by the Municipal League, which is managed with political sense, but each successive defeat was by a larger majority for the machine.

There is no check upon this machine excepting the chance of a mistake, the imminent fear of treachery, and the remote danger of revolt. To meet this last, the machine, as a State organization, has set about throttling public criticism. Ashbridge found that blackmail was ineffective. Durham, Quay, and Governor Pennypacker have passed a libel law which meant to muzzle the press. The Governor was actuated apparently only by his sufferings from cartoons and comments during his campaign; the Philadelphia ring has boodling plans ahead which exposure might make exasperating to the people. The Philadelphia *Press*, the leading Republican organ in the State, puts it right: "The Governor wanted it [the law] in the hope of escaping from the unescapable cartoon. The gang wanted it in hope of muzzling the opposition to jobs. . . . The act is distinctly designed to gag the press in the interest of the plunderers and against the interest of the people."

Disfranchised, without a choice of parties; denied, so the Municipal League declares, the ancient right of petition; and now to lose "free speech,"—is there no hope for Philadelphia? Yes, the Philadelphians have a very present hope. It is in their new mayor, John Weaver. There is nothing in his record to inspire faith in an outsider. He speaks himself of two notorious "miscarriages of justice" during his term as District Attorney; he was the nominee of the ring; and the ring men have confidence in him. But so have the people, and Mr. Weaver makes fair promises. So did Ashbridge. There is this difference, however: Mr. Weaver has made a good start. He compromised with the machine on his appointments, but he declared against the protection of vice, for free voting, and he stopped some "wholesale grabs" or "maces" that appeared in the Legislature, just before he took office.

One was a bill to enable (ring) companies to "appropriate, take, and use all water within this commonwealth and belonging either to public or to private persons as it may require for its private purposes." This was a scheme to sell out the water-works of Philadelphia, and all other such plants in the State. Another bill was to open the way to a seizure of the light and power of the city and of the State. Martin and Warwick "leased" the city gas works. Durham and his crowd wanted a whack at it. "It shall be lawful," the bill read, "for any city, town, or borough owning any gas works or electric light plant for supplying light, heat, and power, to sell, lease, or otherwise dispose of the same to individuals or corporations, and in order to obtain the best possible returns therefor, such municipal body may . . . vest in the lessees or purchasers the exclusive right, both as against such municipal corporations and against any and all other persons and corporations, to supply gas or electricity. . . ." As in St. Louis, the public property of the city is to be sold off. These schemes are to go through later, I am told, but on Mr. Weaver's declarations that he would not "stand for them," they were laid over.

It looks as if the Philadelphians were right about Mr. Weaver, but what if they are? Think of a city putting its whole faith in one man, in the *hope* that John Weaver, an Englishman by birth, will *give* them good government! And why should he do that? Why should he serve the people and not the ring? The ring can make or break him; the people of Philadelphia can neither reward nor punish him. For even if he restores to them their ballots and proves himself a good mayor, he cannot succeed himself; the good charter forbids more than one term.

Chicago: Half Free and Fighting On

(*October, 1903*)

While these articles on municipal corruption were appearing, readers of them were writing to the magazine asking what they, as citizens, were to do about it all. As if I knew; as if "we" knew; as if there were any one way to deal with this problem in all places under any circumstances. There isn't, and if I had gone around with a ready-made reform scheme in the back of my head, it would have served only to keep me from seeing straight the facts that would not support my theory. The only editorial scheme we had was to study a few choice examples of bad city government and tell how the bad was accomplished, then seek out, here and abroad, some typical good governments and explain how the good was done;—not how to do it, mind you, but how it had been done. Though the bad government series was not yet complete, since so many good men apparently want to go to work right off, it was decided to pause for an instance on the reform side. I have chosen the best I have found. Political grafters have been cheerful enough to tell me they have "got lots of pointers" from the corruption articles. I trust the reformers will pick up some "pointers" from—Chicago.

Yes, Chicago. First in violence, deepest in dirt; loud, lawless, unlovely, ill-smelling, irreverent, new; an overgrown gawk of a village, the "tough" among cities, a spectacle for the nation;—I give Chicago no quarter and Chicago asks for none. "Good," they cheer, when you find fault; "give us the gaff. We deserve it and it does us good." They do deserve it. Lying low beside a great lake of pure, cold water, the city has neither enough nor good enough water. With the ingenuity and will to turn their sewer, the Chicago River, and make it run backwards and upwards out of the Lake, the city cannot solve the smoke nuisance. With resources for a magnificent system of public parking, it is too poor to pave and clean the streets. They can balance high buildings on rafts floating in mud, but they can't quench the stench of the stockyards. The enterprise which carried through a World's Fair to a world's triumph is satisfied with two thousand five hundred policemen for two million inhabitants and one hundred and ninety-six square miles of territory, a force so insufficient (and inefficient) that it cannot protect itself, to say nothing of handling mobs, riotous strikers, and the rest of that lawlessness which disgraces Chicago. Though the city has an extra-legal system of controlling vice and crime, which is so effective that the mayor has been able to stop any practices against which he has turned his face—the "panel game," the "hat game," "wine rooms," "safe blowing";—though gambling is limited, regulated, and fair, and prostitution orderly; though, in short, through the power of certain political and criminal leaders—the mayor has been able to make Chicago, criminally speaking, "honest"—burglary and cruel hold-ups are tolerated. As government, all this is preposterous.

But I do not cite Chicago as an example of good municipal government, nor yet of good American municipal government; New York has, for the moment, a much better administration. But neither is Chicago a good example of bad government. There is grafting there, but after St. Louis it seems petty and after Philadelphia most unprofessional. Chicago is interesting for the things it has "fixed." What is wrong there is ridiculous. Politically and morally speaking, Chicago should be celebrated among American cities for reform, real reform, not moral fits and political uprisings, not reform waves that wash the "best people" into office to make fools of themselves and subside leaving the machine stronger than ever,—none of these aristocratic disappointments of popular government,—but reform that reforms, slow, sure, political, democratic reform, by the people, for the people. That is what Chicago has. It has found a way. I don't know that it is *the* way. All that I am sure of is that Chicago has something to teach every city and town in the country—including Chicago.

For Chicago is reformed only in spots. A political map of the city would show a central circle of white with a few white dots and dashes on a background of black, gray, and yellow. But the city once was pretty solid black. Criminally it was wide open; commercially it was brazen; socially it was thoughtless and raw; it was a settlement of individuals and groups and interests with no common city sense and no political conscience. Everybody was for himself, none was for Chicago. There were political parties, but the organizations were controlled by rings, which in turn were parts of State rings, which in turn were backed and used by leading business interests through which this corrupt and corrupting system reached with its ramifications far and high and low into the social organization. The grafting was miscellaneous and very general; but the most open corruption was that which centered in the City Council. It never was well organized and orderly. The aldermen had "combines," leaders, and prices, but, a lot of good-natured honest thieves, they were independent of party bosses and "the organizations," which were busy at their own graft. They were so unbusinesslike that business men went into the City Council to reduce the festival of blackmail to decent and systematic bribery. These men helped matters some, but the happy-go-lucky spirit persisted until the advent of Charles T. Yerkes from Philadelphia, who, with his large experience of Pennsylvania methods, first made boodling a serious business. He had to go right into politics himself to get anything done. But he did get things done. The aldermanic combine was fast selling out the city to its "best citizens," when some decent men spoke up and called upon the people to stop it, the people who alone can stop such things.

And the people of Chicago stopped it; they have beaten boodling. That is about all they have done so far, but that is about all they have tried deliberately and systematically to do, and the way they have done that proves that they can do anything they set out to do. They worry about the rest; half free, they are not half satisfied and not half done. But boodling, with its backing of "big men" and "big interests," is the hardest evil a democracy has to fight, and a people who can beat it can beat anything.

Every community, city, town, village, State—the United States itself—has a certain number of men who are willing, if it doesn't cost anything, to vote right. They don't want to "hurt their business"; they "can't afford the time to go to the primaries"; they don't care to think much. But they will vote. This may not be much, but it is enough. All that this independent, non-partisan vote wants is leadership, and that is what the Chicago reformers furnished.

They had no such definite idea when they began. They had no theory at all—nothing but wrath, experience, common Chicago sense, and newspapers ready to back reform, not for the news, but for the common good. Theories they had tried; and exposures, celebrated trials, even some convictions of boodlers. They had gone in for a civil-service reform law, and, by the way, they got a good one, probably the best in any city in the country. But exposés are good only for one election; court trials may punish individuals, but even convictions do not break up a corrupt system; and a "reform law" without reform citizenship is like a ship without a crew. With all their "reforms," bad government persisted. There was that bear garden—the City Council; something ought to be done to that. Men like William Kent, John H. Hamline, W. R. Manierre, A. W. Maltby, and James R. Mann had gone in there from their "respectable" wards, and their presence proved that they could get there; their speeches were public protests, and their votes, "no," "no," "no," were plain indicators of wrong. But all this was not enough. The

Civic Federation, a respectable but inefficient universal reforming association, met without plans in 1895. It called together two hundred representative men, with Lyman J. Gage at their head, to "do something." The two hundred appointed a committee of fifteen to "find something to do." One of the fifteen drew forth a fully drawn plan for a new municipal party, the old, old scheme. "That won't do," said Edwin Burritt Smith to Mr. Gage, who sat beside him. "No, that won't do," said Gage. But they didn't know what to do. To gain time Mr. Smith moved a sub-committee. The sub-committee reported back to the fifteen, the fifteen to the two hundred. And so, as Mr. Smith said, they "fumbled."

But notice what they didn't do. Fumblers as they were, they didn't talk of more exposures. "Heavens, we know enough," said one. They didn't go to the Legislature for a new charter. They needed one, they need one to-day, and badly, too, but the men who didn't know what, but did know what not to do, wouldn't let them commit the folly of asking one corrupt legislature to legislate another corrupt legislature out of existence. And they didn't wait till the next mayoralty election to elect a "business mayor" who should give them good government.

They were bound to accept the situation just as it was —the laws, the conditions, the political circumstances, all exactly as they were—and, just as a politician would, go into the next fight whatever it was and fight. All they needed was a fighter. So it was moved to find a man, one man, and let this man find eight other men, who should organize the "Municipal Voters' League." There were no instructions; the very name was chosen because it meant nothing and might mean anything.

But the man! That was the problem. There were men,

a few, but the one man is always hard to find. There was William Kent, rich, young, afraid of nothing and always ready, but he was an alderman, and the wise ones declared that the Nine must not only be disinterested, but must appear so. William Kent wouldn't do. Others were suggested; none that would do.

"How about George E. Cole?"

"Just the man," said Mr. Gage, and all knew the thought was an inspiration.

George E. Cole described himself to me as a "second-class business man." Standing about five feet high, he knows he is no taller; but he knows that that is tall enough. Cole is a fighter. Nobody discovered it, perhaps, till he was past his fiftieth year. Then one Martin B. Madden found it out. Madden, a prominent citizen, president of the Western Stone Company, and a man of tremendous political power, was one of the business men who went into the Council to bring order out of the chaos of corruption. He was a Yerkes leader. Madden lived in Cole's ward. His house was in sight of Cole's house. "The sight of it made me hot," said Cole, "for I knew what it represented." Cole had set out to defeat Madden, and he made a campaign which attracted the attention of the whole town. Madden was re-elected, but Cole had proved himself, and that was what made Lyman J. Gage say that Cole was "just the man."

"You come to me as a Hobson's choice," said Mr. Cole to the committee, "as a sort of forlorn hope. All right," he added, "as a last chance, I'll take it."

Cole went out to make up the Nine. He chose William H. Colvin, a wealthy business man, retired; Edwin Burritt Smith, publicist and lawyer; M. J. Carroll, ex-labor leader, ex-typesetter, an editorial writer on a trade journal; Frank

Wells, a well-known real estate man; R. R. Donnelly, the head of one of the greatest printing establishments in the city; and Hoyt King, a young lawyer who turned out to be a natural investigator. These made, with Cole himself, only seven, but he had the help and counsel of Kent, Allen B. Pond, the architect, Judge Murray F. Tuley, Francis Lackner, and Graham Taylor. "We were just a few commonplace, ordinary men," said one of them to me, "and there is your encouragement for other commonplace, ordinary men." These men were selected for what they could do, however, not for what they "represented." The One Hundred, which the Nine were to complete, was to do the representing. But the One Hundred never was completed, and the ward committee, a feature of the first campaign, was abandoned later on. "The boss and the ring" was the model of the Nine, only they did not know it. They were not thinking of principles and methods. Work was their instinct and the fighting has always been thick. The next election was to be held in April, and by the time they were ready February was half over. Since it was to be an election of aldermen, they went right out after the aldermen. There were sixty-eight in all—fifty-seven of them "thieves," as the League reported promptly and plainly. Of the sixty-eight, the terms of thirty-four were expiring, and these all were likely to come up for re-election.

The thing to do was to beat the rascals. But how? Mr. Cole and his committee were pioneers; they had to blaze the way, and, without plans, they set about it directly. Seeking votes, and honest votes, with no organization to depend upon, they had to have publicity. "We had first to let people know we were there," said Cole, so he stepped "out into the lime-light" and, with his short legs apart, his weak eyes blinking, he talked. The League was out to beat the boodlers up for re-election, he said, with much picturesque English. Now Chicago is willing to have anybody try to do anything worth while in Chicago; no matter who you are or where you come from, Chicago will give you a cheer and a first boost. When, therefore, George E. Cole stood up and said he and a quiet little committee were going to beat some politicians at the game of politics, the good-natured town said: "All right, go ahead and beat 'em; but how?" Cole was ready with his answer. "We're going to publish the records of the thieves who want to get back at the trough." Alderman Kent and his decent colleagues produced the records of their indecent colleagues, and the League announced that of the thirty-four retiring aldermen, twenty-six were rogues. Hoyt King and a staff of briefless young lawyers looked up war records, and "these also we will publish," said Cole. And they did; the Chicago newspapers, long on the right side and ever ready, printed them, and they were "mighty interesting reading." Edwin Burritt Smith stated the facts; Cole added "ginger," and Kent "pepper and salt and vinegar." They soon had publicity. Some of the committee shrank from the worst of it, but Cole stood out and took it. He became a character in the town. He was photographed and caricatured; he was "Boss Cole" and "Old King Cole," but all was grist to this reform mill. Some of the retiring aldermen retired at once. Others were retired. If information turned up by Hoyt King was too private for publication, the committee was, and is to-day, capable of sending for the candidate and advising him to get off the ticket. This was called "blackmail," and I will call it that, if the word will help anybody to appreciate how hard these reform politicians played and play the game.

While they were talking, however, they were working, and their work was done in the wards. Each ward was separately studied, the politics of each was separately understood, and separately each ward was fought. Declaring only for "aggressive honesty" at first, not competence, they did not stick even to that. They wanted to beat the rascals that were in, and, if necessary, if they couldn't hope to elect an honest man, they helped a likely rascal to beat the rascal that was in and known. They drew up a pledge of loyalty to public interest, but they didn't insist on it in some cases. Like the politicians, they were opportunists. Like the politicians, too, they were non-partisans. They played off one party against another, or, if the two organizations hung together, they put up an independent. They broke many a cherished reform principle, but few rules of practical politics. Thus, while they had some of their own sort of men nominated, they did not attempt, they did not think of running "respectable" or "business" candidates as such. Neither were they afraid to dicker with ward leaders and "corrupt politicians." They went down into the ward, urged the minority organization leader to name a "good man," on promise of independent support, then campaigned against the majority nominee with circulars, house-to-house canvassers, mass-meetings, bands, speakers, and parades. I should say that the basic unstated principle of this reform movement, struck out early in the practice of the Nine, was to let the politicians rule, but through better and better men whom the Nine forced upon them with public opinion. But again I want to emphasize the fact that they had no fine-spun theories and no definite principles beyond that of being always for the best available man. They were with the Democrats in one ward, with the Republicans in another, but in none were they respecters of persons.

Right here appeared that insidious influence which we have seen defeating or opposing reform in other cities—the interference of respectable men to save their friends. In the Twenty-second Ward the Democrats nominated a director (now deceased) of the First National Bank and a prominent man socially and financially. John Colvin, one of the "Big Four," a politician who had gone away rich to Europe and was returning to go back into politics, also was running. The League preferred John Maynard Harlan, a son of Justice Harlan, and they elected him. The bank of which the respectable Democratic candidate was a director was the bank of which Lyman J. Gage, of the League, was president. All that the League had against this man was that he was the proprietor of a house leased for questionable purposes, and his friends, including Mr. Gage, were highly indignant. Mr. Gage pleaded and protested. The committee was "sick of pulls" and they made short work of this most "respectable" pull. They had "turned down" politicians on no better excuse, and they declared they were not going to overlook in the friend of their friends what they condemned in some poor devil who had no friends.

There were many such cases, then and later; this sort of thing has never ceased and it never will cease; reform must always "go too far," if it is to go at all, for it is up there in the "too far" that corruption has its source. The League, by meeting it early, and "spotting it," as Mr. Cole said, not only discouraged such interference, but fixed its own character and won public confidence. For everything in those days was open. The League works more quietly now, but then Cole was talking it all out, plain to the verge of brutality, forcible to the limit of language, and honest to utter ruthlessness. He blundered and they all made mistakes, but their blundering only helped them, for while the errors were plain errors, the fairness of mind that rejected an Edward M. Stanwood, for example, was plain too. Stanwood, a respectable business man, had served as alderman, but his re-election was advised against by the League because he had "voted with the gang." A high public official, three judges, and several other prominent men interceded on the ground that "in every instance where he is charged with having voted for a so-called boodle ordinance, it was not done corruptly, but that he might secure votes for some meritorious measure." The League answered in this style: "We regard this defense, which is put forward with confidence by men of your standing, as painful evidence of the low standard by which the public conduct of city officials has come to be measured by good citizens. Do you not know that this is one of the most insidious and common forms of legislative corruption?" Mr. Stanwood was defeated.

The League "made good." Of the twenty-six outgoing aldermen with bad records, sixteen were not renominated. Of the ten who were, four were beaten at the polls. The League's recommendations were followed in twenty-five wards; they were disregarded in five; in some wards no fight was made.

A victory so extraordinary would have satisfied some reformers. Others would have been inflated by it and ruined. These men became canny. They chose this propitious moment to get rid of the committee of One Hundred respectables. Such a body is all very well to launch a reform, when no one knows that it is going to do serious work; but, as the Cole committee had learned, representative men with many interests can be reached. The little committee incorporated the League, then called together the big committee, congratulated it, and proposed a constitution and by-laws which would throw all the work—and all the power—to the little committee. The little committee was to call on the big committee only as money or some "really important" help was needed. The big committee approved, swelled up, adjourned, and that is the last time it has ever met.

Thus free of "pulls," gentlemanly pulls, but pulls just the same, the "nine" became nine by adding two—Allen B. Pond and Francis Lackner—and prepared for the next campaign. Their aldermen, the "reform crowd," in the City Council were too few to do anything alone, but they could protest, and they did. They adopted the system of William Kent, which was to find out what was going on and tell it in Council meetings.

"If you go on giving away the people's franchises like this," Alderman Harlan would say, "you may wake up some morning to find street lamps are useful for other purposes than lighting the streets." Or, "Some night the citizens, who are watching you, may come down here from the galleries with pieces of hemp in their hands." Then he would picture an imagined scene of the galleries rising and coming down upon the floor. He made his descriptions so vivid and creepy that they made some aldermen fidget. "I don't like dis business all about street lamps and hemp—vot dot is?" said a German boodler one night. "We don't come here for no such a business."

"We meant only to make head-lines for the papers," said one of the reform aldermen. "If we could keep the attention of the public upon the Council we could make clear what was going on there, and that would put meaning into our next campaign. And we certainly did fill the galleries and the newspapers."

As a matter of fact, however, they did much more. They developed in that year the issue which has dominated Chicago local politics ever since—the proper compensation to the city for public franchises. These valuable rights should not be given away, they declared, and they repeated it for good measures as well as bad. Not only must the city be paid, but public convenience and interest must be safeguarded. The boodlers boodled and the franchises went off; the protestation hurried the rotten business; but even that haste helped the cause. For the sight, week after week, of the boodle raids by rapacious capital fixed public opinion, and if the cry raised then for municipal ownership ever becomes a fact in Chicago, capital can go back to those days and blame itself.

Most of the early Chicago street railway franchises were limited, carelessly, to twenty-five years—the first one in 1858. In 1883, when the earliest franchises might have been terminated, the Council ventured to pass only a blanket extension for twenty years—till July 30, 1903. This was well enough for Chicago financiers, but in 1886-87, when Yerkes appeared, with Widener and Elkins behind him, and bought up the West and North Side companies, he applied Pennsylvania methods. He pushed bills through the Legislature, saw them vetoed by Governor Altgeld, set about having his own Governor next time, and in 1897 got, not all that he wanted (for the people of Illinois are not like the people of Pennsylvania), but the Allen bill, which would do—if the Chicago City Council of 1897 would give it force.

The Municipal Voters' League had begun its second campaign in December, 1896, with the publication of the records of the retiring aldermen, the second half of the old body, and, though this was before the Allen bill was passed, Yerkes was active, and his men were particularized. As the campaign progressed the legislation at Springfield gave it point and local developments gave it breadth. It was a mayoralty year, and Alderman John Maynard Harlan had himself nominated on an independent, non-partisan ticket. "Bobbie" Burke, the Democratic boss, brought forward Carter H. Harrison, and the Republicans nominated Judge Nathaniel C. Sears. Harrison at that time was known only as the son of his father. Sears was a fine man; but neither of these had seized the street railway issue. Mr. Harlan stood on that, and he made a campaign which is talked about to this day in Chicago. It was brilliant. He had had the ear of the town through the newspaper reports of his tirades in the Council, and the people went to hear him now as night after night he arraigned, not the bribed legislators, but the rich bribers. Once he called the roll of street railway directors and asked each what he was doing while his business was being boodled through the State Legislature. Earnest, eloquent, honest, he was witty too. Yerkes called him an ass. "If Yerkes will consult his Bible," said Harlan, "he will learn that great things have been done with the jaw-bone of an ass." This young man had no organization (the League confined itself to the aldermen); it was a speaking campaign; but he caught the spirit of Chicago, and in the last week men say you could feel the drift of sentiment to him. Though he was defeated, he got 70,000 votes, 10,000 more than the regular Republican candidate, and elected Harrison. And his campaign not only phrased the traction issue in men's minds; it is said to have taught young Mayor Harrison the use of it. At any rate, Harrison and Chicago have been safe on the city's side of it ever since.

The League also won on it. They gave bad records to twenty-seven of the thirty-four outgoing aldermen. Fifteen were not renominated. Of the twelve who ran again, nine were beaten. This victory gave them a solid third of the Council. The reform crowd combined with Mayor Harrison, the President of the Council, and his followers, and defeated ordinances introduced to give effect to Yerkes's odious Allen law.

Here again the League might have retired in glory, but these "commonplace, ordinary men" proposed instead that they go ahead and get a majority, organize the Council on a non-partisan basis, and pass from a negative, anti-boodling policy to one of positive, constructive legislation. This meant also to advance from "beating bad men" to the "election of good men," and as for the good men, the standard was to be raised from mere honesty to honesty and efficiency too. With such high purposes in view, the Nine went into their third campaign. They had to condemn men they had recommended in their first year, but "we are always ready to eat dirt," they say. They pointed to the franchise issue, called for men capable of coping with the railways, and with bands playing, orators shouting, and Cole roaring like a sea-captain, they made the campaign of 1898 the hottest in their history. It nearly killed some of them, but they "won out"; the League had a nominal majority of the City Council.

Then came their first bitter disappointment. They failed to organize the aldermen. They tried, and were on the verge of success, when defeat came, a most significant defeat. The League had brought into political life some new men, shop-keepers and small business men, all with perfect records, or none. They were men who meant well, but business is no training for politics; the shop-keepers who knew how to resist the temptations of trade were untried in those of politics, and the boodle gang "bowled them over like little tin soldiers." They were persuaded that it was no more than right to "let the dominant party make up committees and run the Council"; that was "usage," and, what with bribery, sophistry, and flattery, the League was beaten by its weak friends. The real crisis in the League had come.

Mr. Cole resigned. He took the view that the League work was done; it could do no more; his health was suffering and his business was going to the dogs. The big corporations, the railroads, great business houses and their friends, had taken their business away from him. But this boycott had begun in the first campaign and Cole had met it with the declaration that he didn't "care a d—n." "I have a wife and a boy," he said. "I want their respect. The rest can all go to h—l." Cole has organized since a league to reform the Legislature, but after the 1898 campaign the Nine were tired, disappointed, and Cole was temporarily used up.

The Nine had to let Cole and Hoyt King go. But they wouldn't let the League go. They had no successor for Cole. None on the committee would take his place; they all declined it in turn. They looked outside for a man, finding nobody. The prospect was dark. Then William Kent spoke up. Kent had time and money, but he wouldn't do anything anyone else could be persuaded to do. He was not strong physically, and his physicians had warned him that to live he must work little and play much. At that moment he was under orders to go West and shoot. But when he saw what was happening, he said:

"I'm not the man for this job; I'm no organizer. I can smash more things in a minute than I can build up in a hundred years. But the League has got to go on, so I'll take Cole's place if you'll give me a hard-working, able man for secretary, an organizer and a master of detail."

Such a secretary was hard to find, but Allen B. Pond, the architect, a man made for fine work, took this rough-and-tumble task. And these two with the committee strengthened and active, not only held their own, they not only met the receding wave of reactionary sentiment against reform, but they made progress. In 1899 they won a clear majority of the Council, pledged their men before election to a non-partisan organization of the Council, and were in shape for constructive legislation. In 1900 they increased their majority, but they did not think it necessary to bind candidates before the election to the non-partisan-committees plan, and the Republicans organized the house. This party maintained the standard of the committees; there was no falling off there, but that was not the point. Parties were recognized in the Council, and the League had hoped for only one line of demarcation: special interests versus the interests of the city. During the time of Kent and Pond, however, the power for good of the League was established, the question of its permanency settled, and the use of able, conscientious aldermen recognized. The public opinion it developed and pointed held the Council so steady that, with Mayor

Harrison and his personal following among the Democrats on that side, the aldermen refused to do anything for the street railway companies until the Allen bill was repealed. And, all ready to pass anything at Springfield, Yerkes had to permit the repeal, and he soon after closed up his business in Chicago and went away to London, where he is said to be happy and prosperous.

The first time I went to Chicago, to see what form of corruption they had, I found there was something the matter with the political machinery. There was the normal plan of government for a city, rings with bosses, and grafting business interests behind. Philadelphia, Pittsburg, St. Louis, are all governed on such a plan. But in Chicago it didn't work. "Business" was at a standstill and business was suffering. What was the matter? I beleaguered the political leaders with questions: "Why didn't the politicians control? What was wrong with the machines?" The "boss" defended the organizations, blaming the people. "But the people could be fooled by any capable politician," I demurred. The boss blamed the reformers. "Reformers!" I exclaimed. "I've seen some of your reformers. They aren't different from reformers elsewhere, are they?" "No," he said, well pleased. But when I concluded that it must then be the weakness of the Chicago bosses, his pride cried out. "Say," he said, "have you seen that blankety-blank Fisher?"

I hadn't, I said. "Well, you want to," he said, and I went straightway and saw Fisher—Mr. Walter L. Fisher, secretary of the Municipal Voters' League. Then it was that I began to understand the Chicago political situation. Fisher was a reformer: an able young lawyer of independent means, a mind ripe with high purposes and ideals, self-confident, high-minded, conclusive. He showed me an orderly bureau of indexed information, such as I had seen before. He outlined the scheme of the Municipal Voters' League, all in a bored, polite, familiar way. There was no light in him nor anything new or vital in his reform as he described it. It was all incomprehensible till I asked him how he carried the Seventeenth Ward, a mixed and normally Democratic ward, in one year for a Republican by some 1300 plurality, the next year for a Democrat by some 1800, the third for a Republican again. His face lighted up, a keen, shrewd look came into his eyes, and he said: "I did not carry that ward; its own people did it, but I'll tell you how it was managed." And he told me a story that was politics. I asked about another ward, and he told me the story of that. It was entirely different, but it, too, was politics. Fisher is a politician—with the education, associations, and the idealism of the reformers who fail, this man has cunning, courage, tact, and, rarer still, faith in the people. In short, reform in Chicago has such a leader as corruption alone usually has; a first-class executive mind and a natural manager of men.

When, after the aldermanic campaign of 1900, Messrs. Kent and Pond resigned as president and secretary of the League's executive committee, Charles R. Crane and Mr. Fisher succeeded in their places. Mr. Crane is a man with an international business, which takes him often to Russia, but he comes back for the Chicago aldermanic campaigns. He leaves the game to Mr. Fisher, and says Fisher is the man, but Crane is a backer of great force and of persistent though quiet activity. These two, with a picked committee of experienced and sensible men—Pond, Kent, Smith, Frank H. Scott, Graham Taylor, Sigmund Zeisler, and Lessing Rosenthal—took the League as an established institution, perfected its system, opened a head quarters for work the year around; and this force, Mr. Fisher, with his political genius, has made a factor of the first rank in practical politics. Fisher made fights in the "hopeless" wards, and won them. He has raised the reform majority in the City Council to two-thirds; he has lifted the standard of aldermen from honesty to a gradually rising scale of ability, and in his first year the Council was organized on a non-partisan basis. This feature of municipal reform is established now, by the satisfaction of the aldermen themselves with the way it works. And a most important feature it is, too. "We have four shots at every man headed for the Council," said one of the League—"one with his record when his term expires; another when he is up for the nomination; a third when he is running as a candidate; the fourth when the committees are formed. If he is bad he is put on a minority in a strong committee; if he is doubtful, with a weak or doubtful majority on an important committee with a strong minority—a minority so strong that they can let him show his hand, then beat him with a minority report." Careful not to interfere in legislation, the League keeps a watch on every move in the Council. Cole started this. He used to sit in the gallery every meeting night, but under Crane and Fisher, an assistant secretary—first Henry B. Chamberlain, now George C. Sikes—has followed the daily routine of committee work as well as the final meetings.

Fisher has carried the early practice of meeting politicians on their own ground to a very practical extreme. When tact and good humor failed, he applied force. Thus, when he set about preparing a year ahead for his fights in unpromising wards, he sent to the ward leaders on both sides for their lists of captains, lieutenants, and heelers. They refused, with expressions of astonishment at his "gall." Mr. Chamberlain directed a most searching investigation of the wards, precinct by precinct, block by block, and not only gathered a rich fund of information, but so frightened the politicians who heard of the inquiries that many of them came around and gave up their lists. Whether these helped or not, however, the wards were studied, and it was by such information and undermining political work, combined with skill and a fearless appeal to the people of the ward, that Fisher beat out with Hubert W. Butler the notorious Henry Wulff, an ex-State Treasurer, in the ward convention of Wulff's own party, and then defeated Wulff, who ran as an independent, at the polls.

Such experience won the respect of the politicians, as well as their fear, and in 1902 and 1903 the worst of them, or the best, came personally to Fisher to see what they could do. He was their equal in "the game of talk," they found, and their superior in tactics, for when he could not persuade them to put up good men and "play fair," he measured himself with them in strategy. Thus one day "Billy" Loeffler, the Democratic leader in the Democratic Ninth Ward, asked Mr. Fisher if the League did not want to name the Democratic candidate for alderman in his ward. Loeffler's business partner, "Hot Stove" Brenner, was running on the Republican ticket and Fisher knew that the Democratic organization would pull for Brenner. But Fisher accepted what was a challenge to political play and suggested Michael J. Preib. Loeffler was dazed at the name; it was new to him, but he accepted the man and nominated him. The Ninth is a strong Hebrew ward. To draw off the Republican and Jewish vote from Brenner, Fisher procured the nomination as an independent of Jacob Diamond, a popular young Hebrew, and he backed him too, intending, as he told both Preib and Diamond, to prefer in the end the one that should develop the greater strength. Meanwhile the League watched Loeffler. He was quietly throwing his support from Preib to Brenner. Five days before election it was clear that, though Diamond had developed unexpected strength, Preib was stronger. Fisher went to Loeffler and accused him of not doing all he could for Preib. Loeffler declared he was. Fisher proposed a letter from Loeffler to his personal friends asking them to vote for Preib. Loeffler hesitated, but he signed one that Fisher dictated. Loeffler advised the publication of the statement in the Jewish papers, and, though he consented to have it mailed to voters, he thought it "an unnecessary expense." When Fisher got back to the League headquarters, he rushed off copies of the letter through the mails to all the voters in the ward. By the time Loeffler heard of this it was too late to do anything; he tried, but he never caught up with those letters. His partner, Brenner, was defeated.

A politician? A boss. Chicago has in Walter L. Fisher a reform boss, and in the Nine of the Municipal Voters' League, with their associated editors and able finance and advisory committees, a reform ring. They have no machine, no patronage, no power that they can abuse. They haven't even a list of their voters. All they have is the confidence of the anonymous honest men of Chicago who care more for Chicago than for anything else. This they have won by a long record of good judgments, honest, obvious devotion to the public good, and a disinterestedness which has avoided even individual credit; not a hundred men in the city could name the Committee of Nine.

Working wide open at first, when it was necessary, they have withdrawn more and more ever since, and their policy now is one of dignified silence except when a plain statement of facts is required; then they speak as the League, simply, directly, but with human feeling, and leave their following of voters to act with or against them as they please. I have laid great stress on the technical, political skill of Fisher and the Nine, not because that is their chief reliance; it isn't: the study and the enlightenment of public opinion is their great function and force. But other reform organizations have tried this way. These reformers have, with the newspapers and the aldermen, not only done it thoroughly and persistently; they have not only developed an educated citizenship; they have made it an effective force, effective in legislation and in practical politics. In short: political reform, politically conducted, has produced reform politicians working for the reform of the city with the methods of politics. They do everything that a politician does, except buy votes and sell them. They play politics in the interest of the city.

And what has the city got out of it? Many things, but at least one great spectacle to show the world, the political spectacle of the year, and it is still going on. The properly accredited representatives of two American city railway companies are meeting in the open with a regular committee of an American board of aldermen, and they are negotiating for the continuance of certain street railway franchises on terms fair both to the city and to the corporations, without a whisper of bribery, with composure, reasonableness, knowledge (on the aldermen's part, long-studied information and almost expert knowledge); with an eye to the future, to the just profit of the railways, and the convenience of the people of the city. This in an American city—in Chicago!

Those franchises which Yerkes tried to "fix" expired on

July 30. There was a dispute about that, and the railways were prepared to fight. One is a Chicago corporation held by Chicago capital, and the men in it knew the conditions. The other belongs to New York and Philadelphia capitalists, whom Yerkes got to hold it when he gave up and went away; they couldn't understand. This "foreign" capital sent picked men out to Chicago to "fight." One of the items said to have been put in their bill of appropriation was "For use in Chicago—$1,000,000." Their local officers and directors and friends warned them to "go slow."

"Do you mean to tell us," said the Easterners, "that we can't do in Chicago what we have done in Philadelphia, New York, and——"

"That's exactly what we mean," was the answer.

Incredulous, they did do some such "work." They had the broken rings with them, and the "busted bosses," and they had the city on the hip in one particular. Though the franchises expired, the city had no authority in law to take over the railways and had to get it from Springfield. The Republican ring, with some Democratic following, had organized the Legislature on an explicit arrangement that "no traction legislation should pass in 1903." The railways knew they couldn't get any; all they asked was that the city shouldn't have any either. It was a political game, but Chicago was sure that two could play at it. Harrison was up for re-election; he was right on traction. The Republicans nominated a business man, Graeme Stewart, who also pledged himself. Then they all went to Springfield, and, with the whole city and State looking on, the city's reform politicians beat the regulars. The city's bill was buried in committee, but to make a showing for Stewart the Republican ring had to pass some sort of a bill. They offered a poor substitute. With the city against it, the Speaker "gaveled it through" amid a scene of the wildest excitement. He passed the bill, but he was driven from his chair, and the scandal compelled him and the ring to reconsider that bill and pass the city's own enabling act.

Both the traction companies had been interested in this Springfield fiasco; they had been working together, but the local capitalists did not like the business. They soon offered to settle separately, and went into session with the city's lawyers, Edwin Burritt Smith, of the League, and John C. Mathis. The Easterners' representatives, headed by a "brilliant" New York lawyer, had to negotiate too. Their brilliant lawyer undertook to "talk sense" into the aldermanic committee. This committee had been out visiting all the large Eastern cities, studying the traction situations everywhere; on their own account they had had drawn for them one of the most complete reports ever made for a city by an expert. Moreover, they knew the law and the finances of the traction companies, better far than the New York lawyers. When, therefore, the brilliant legal light had made one of his smooth, elaborate speeches, some hard-headed alderman would get up and say that he "gathered and gleaned" thus and so from the last speaker; he wasn't quite sure, but if thus and so was what the gentleman from New York had said, then it looked to him like tommy rot. Then the lawyer would spin another web, only to have some other commonplace-looking alderman tear it to pieces. Those lawyers were dumfounded. They were advised to see Fisher. They saw Fisher.

"You are welcome, if you wish," he is said to have said, "to talk foolishness, but I advise you to stop it. I do not speak for the Council, but I think I know what it will say when it speaks for itself. Those aldermen know their business. They know sense and they know nonsense. They can't be fooled. If you go at them with reason they will go a long way toward helping you. However, you shall do as you please about this. But let me burn this one thing in upon your consciousness: Don't try money on them or anybody else. They will listen to your nonsense with patience, but if we hear of you trying to bribe anybody—an alderman or a politician or a newspaper or a reporter—all negotiations will cease instantly. And nobody will attempt to blackmail you, no one."

This seems to me to be the highest peak of reform. Here is a gentleman, speaking with the authority of absolute faith and knowledge, assuring the representatives of a corporation that it can have all that is due it from a body of aldermen by the expenditure of nothing more than reason. I have heard many a business man say such a condition of things would be hailed by his kind with rejoicing. How do they like it in Chicago? They don't like it at all. I spent one whole forenoon calling on the presidents of banks, great business men, and financiers interested in public utility companies. With all the evidence I had had in other places that these men are the chief sources of corruption, I was unprepared for the sensation of that day. Those financial leaders of Chicago were "mad." All but one of them became so enraged as they talked that they could not behave decently. They rose up, purple in the face, and cursed reform. They said it had hurt business; it had hurt the town. "Anarchy," they called it; "socialism." They named corporations that had left the city; they named others that had planned to come there and had gone elsewhere. They offered me facts and figures to prove that the city was damaged.

"But isn't the reform council honest?" I asked.

"Honest! Yes, but—oh, h—l!"

"And do you realize that all you say means that you regret the passing of boodle and would prefer to have back the old corrupt Council?"

That brought a curse, or a shrewd smile, or a cynical laugh, but that they regretted the passing of the boodle régime is the fact, bitter, astonishing,—but natural enough. We have seen those interests at their bribery in Philadelphia and St. Louis; we have seen them opposing reforms in every city. Here in Chicago we have them cursing reform triumphant, for, though reform may have been a benefit to the city as a community of freemen, it is really bad; it has hurt their business!

Chicago has paid dearly for its reform, and reformers elsewhere might as well realize that if they succeed, their city will pay, too, at first. Capital will boycott it and capital will give it a bad name. The bankers who offered me proof of their losses were offering me material to write down the city. And has Chicago had conspicuous credit for reform? No, it is in ill-repute, "anarchistic," "socialistic" (a commercial term for municipal ownership); it is "unfriendly to capital." But Chicago knows what it is after and it knows the cost. There are business men there who are willing to pay; they told me so. There are business men on the executive and finance committees of the League and others helping outside who are among the leaders of Chicago's business and its bar. Moreover, there are promoters who expect to like an honest Council. One such told me that he meant to apply for franchises shortly, and he believed that, though it would take longer than bribery to negotiate fair terms with aldermen who were keen to safeguard the city's interests, yet business could be done on that basis. "Those reform aldermen are slow, but they are fair," he said.

The aldermen are fair. Exasperated as they have been by the trifling, the trickery, and past boodling of the street railways, inconvenienced by bad service, beset by corporation temptations, they are fairer to-day than the corporations. They have the street railways now in a corner. The negotiations are on, and they could squeeze them with a vengeance. What is the spirit of those aldermen? "Well," said one to me, "I'll tell you how we feel. We've got to get the city's interests well protected. That's first. But we've got more to do than that. They're shy of us; these capitalists don't know how to handle us. They are not up to the new, reform, on-the-level way of doing business. We've got to show capital that we will give them all that is coming to them, and just a little more—a little more, just to get them used to being honest." This was said without a bit of humor, with some anxiety but no bitterness, and not a word about socialism or "confiscating municipal ownership"; that's a "capitalistic" bugaboo. Again, one Saturday night a personal friend of mine who had lost a half-holiday at a conference with some of the leading aldermen, complained of their "preciseness." "First," he said, "they had to have every trivial interest of the city protected, then, when we seemed to be done, they turned around and argued like corporation lawyers for the protection of the corporation."

Those Chicago aldermen are an honor to the country! Men like Jackson and Mavor, Herrmann and Werno, would be a credit to any legislative body in the land, but there is no such body in the land where they could do more good or win more honor. I believe capital will some day prefer to do business with them than with blackmailers and boodlers anywhere.

When that day comes the aldermen will share the credit with the Municipal Voters' League, but all the character and all the ability of both Council and League will not explain the reform of Chicago. The citizens of that city will take most of the glory. They will have done it, as they have done it so far.

Some of my critics have declared they could not believe there was so much difference in the character of communities as I have described. How can they account, then, for Chicago? The people there have political parties, they are partisans. But they know how to vote. Before the League was started, the records show them shifting their vote to the confusion of well-laid political plans. So they have always had bosses, and they have them now, but these bosses admit that they "can't boss Chicago." I think this is partly their fault. William Lorimer, the dominant Republican boss, with whom I talked for an hour one day, certainly does not make the impression, either as a man or as a politician, that Croker makes, or Durham of Philadelphia. But an outsider may easily go wrong on a point like this, and we may leave the credit where they lay it, with the people of Chicago. Fisher is a more forceful man than any of the regulars, and, as a politician, compares with well-known leaders in any city; but Fisher's power is the people's. His leadership may have done much, but there is something else deeper and bigger behind him. At the last aldermanic election, when he discovered on the Saturday before election that the League was recommending, against a bad Democrat, a worse

Republican, he advised the people of that ward to vote for the Socialist; and the people did vote for the Socialist, and they elected him. Again, there is the press, the best in any of our large cities. There are several newspapers in Chicago which have served always the public interest, and their advice is taken by their readers. These editors wield, as they wielded before the League came, that old-fashioned power of the press which is supposed to have passed away. Indeed, one of the finest exhibitions of disinterestedness in this whole reform story was that of these newspapers giving up the individual power and credit which their influence on public opinion gave them, to the League, behind which they stepped to get together and gain for the city what they lost themselves. But this paid them. They did not do it with that motive; they did it for the city, but the city has recognized the service, as another fact shows: There are bad papers in Chicago—papers that serve special interests—and these don't pay.

The agents of reform have been many and efficient, but back of them all was an intelligent, determined people, and they have decided. The city of Chicago is ruled by the citizens of Chicago. Then why are the citizens of Chicago satisfied with half-reform? Why have they reformed the Council and left the administrative side of government so far behind? "One thing at a time," they will tell you out there, and it is wonderful to see them patient after seven years of steadfast, fighting reform.

But that is not the reason. The administration has been improved. It is absurdly backward and uneven; the fire department is excellent, the police is a disgrace, the law department is expert, the health bureau is corrupt, and the street cleaning is hardly worth mention. All this is Carter H. Harrison. He is an honest man personally, but indolent; a shrewd politician, and a character with reserve power, but he has no initial energy. Without ideals, he does only what is demanded of him. He does not seem to know wrong is wrong, till he is taught; nor to care, till criticism arouses his political sense of popular requirement. That sense is keen, but think of it: Every time Chicago wants to go ahead a foot, it has first to push its mayor up inch by inch. In brief, Chicago is a city that wants to be led, and Carter Harrison, with all his political ambition, honest willingness, and obstinate independence, simply follows it. The League leads, and its leaders understand their people. Then why does the League submit to Harrison? Why doesn't the League recommend mayors as well as aldermen? It may some day; but, setting out by accident to clean the Council, stop the boodling, and settle the city railway troubles, they have been content with Mayor Harrison because he had learned his lesson on that. And, I think, as they say the mayor thinks, that when the people of Chicago get the city railways running with enough cars and power; when they have put a stop to boodling forever; they will take up the administrative side of the government. A people who can support for seven years one movement toward reform, should be able to go on forever. With the big boodle beaten, petty political grafting can easily be stopped. All that will be needed then will be a mayor who understands and represents the city; he will be able to make Chicago as rare an example of good government as it is now of reform; which will be an advertisement; good business; it will *pay.*

Post Scriptum, December, 1903.—Chicago has taken up since administrative graft. The Council is conducting an investigation which is showing the city government to have been a second Minneapolis. Mayor Harrison is helping, and the citizens are interested. There is little doubt that Chicago will be cleaned up.

New York: Good Government to the Test

(*November, 1903*)

Just about the time this article will appear, Greater New York will be holding a local election on what has come to be a national question—good government. No doubt there will be other "issues." At this writing (September 15) the candidates were not named nor the platforms written, but the regular politicians hate the main issue, and they have a pretty trick of confusing the honest mind and splitting the honest vote by raising "local issues" which would settle themselves under prolonged honest government. So, too, there will probably be some talk about the effect this election might have upon the next Presidential election; another clever fraud which seldom fails to work to the advantage of rings and grafters, and to the humiliation and despair of good citizenship. We have nothing to do with these deceptions. They may count in New York, they may determine the result, but let them. They are common moves in the corruptionist's game, and, therefore, fair tests of citizenship, for honesty is not the sole qualification for an honest voter; intelligence has to play a part, too, and a little intelligence would defeat all such tricks. Anyhow, they cannot disturb us. I am writing too far ahead, and my readers, for the most part, will be reading too far away to know or care anything about them. We can grasp firmly the essential issues involved and then watch with equanimity the returns for the answer, plain yes or no, which New York will give to the only questions that concern us all: *

Do we Americans really want good government? Do we know it when we see it? Are we capable of that sustained good citizenship which alone can make democracy a success? Or, to save our pride, one other: Is the New York way the right road to permanent reform?

For New York has good government, or, to be more precise, it has a good administration. It is not a question there of turning the rascals out and putting the honest men into their places. The honest men are in, and this election is to decide whether they are to be kept in, which is a very different matter. Any people is capable of rising in wrath to overthrow bad rulers. Philadelphia has done that in its day. New York has done it several times. With fresh and present outrages to avenge, particular villains to punish, and the mob sense of common anger to excite, it is an emotional gratification to go out with the crowd and "smash something." This is nothing but revolt, and even monarchies have uprisings to the credit of their subjects. But revolt is not reform, and one revolutionary ad-

* Tammany tried to introduce national issues, but failed, and "good government" was practically the only question raised.

ministration is not good government. That we free Americans are capable of such assertions of our sovereign power, we have proven; our lynchers are demonstrating it every day. That we can go forth singly also, and, without passion, with nothing but mild approval and dull duty to impel us, vote intelligently to sustain a fairly good municipal government, remains to be shown. And that is what New York has the chance to show; New York, the leading exponent of the great American anti-bad government movement for good government.

According to this, the standard course of municipal reform, the politicians are permitted to organize a party on national lines, take over the government, corrupt and deceive the people, and run things for the private profit of the boss and his ring, till the corruption becomes rampant and a scandal. Then the reformers combine the opposition: the corrupt and unsatisfied minority, the disgruntled groups of the majority, the reform organizations; they nominate a mixed ticket, headed by a "good business man" for mayor, make a "hot campaign" against the government with "Stop, thief!" for the cry, and make a "clean sweep." Usually, this effects only the disciplining of the reckless grafters and the improvement of the graft system of corrupt government. The good mayor turns out to be weak or foolish or "not so good." The politicians "come it over him," as they did over the business mayors who followed the "Gas Ring" revolt in Philadelphia, or the people become disgusted as they did with Mayor Strong, who was carried into office by the anti-Tammany rebellion in New York after the Lexow exposures. Philadelphia gave up after its disappointment, and that is what most cities do. The repeated failures of revolutionary reform to accomplish more than the strengthening of the machine have so discredited this method that wide-awake reformers in several cities—Pittsburg, Cincinnati, Cleveland, Detroit, Minneapolis, and others—are following the lead of Chicago.

The Chicago plan does not depend for success upon any one man or any one year's work, nor upon excitement or any sort of bad government. The reformers there have no ward organizations, no machine at all; their appeal is solely to the intelligence of the voter and their power rests upon that. This is democratic and political, not bourgeois and business reform, and it is interesting to note that whereas reformers elsewhere are forever seeking to concentrate all the powers in the mayor, those of Chicago talk of stripping the mayor to a figurehead and giving his powers to the aldermen who directly represent the people, and who change year by year.

The Chicago way is but one way, however, and a new one, and it must be remembered that this plan has not yet produced a good administration. New York has that. Chicago, after seven years' steady work, has a body of aldermen honest enough and competent to defend the city's interests against boodle capital, but that is about all; it has a wretched administration. New York has stuck to the old way. Provincial and self-centered, it hardly knows there is any other. Chicago laughs and other cities wonder, but never mind, New York, by persistence, has at last achieved a good administration. Will the New Yorkers continue it? That is the question. What Chicago has, it has secure. Its independent citizenship is trained to vote every time and to vote for uninteresting, good aldermen. New York has an independent vote of 100,000, a decisive minority, but the voters have been taught to vote only once in a long while, only when excited by picturesque leadership and sensational exposures, only *against*. New York has been so far an anti-bad government, anti-Tammany, not a good-government town. Can it vote, without Tammany in to incite it, for a good mayor? I think this election, which will answer this question, should decide other cities how to go about reform.

The administration of Mayor Seth Low may not have been perfect, not in the best European sense: not expert, not co-ordinated, certainly not wise. Nevertheless, for an American city, it has been not only honest, but able, undeniably one of the best in the whole country. Some of the departments have been dishonest; others have been so inefficient that they made the whole administration ridiculous. But what of that? Corruption also is clumsy and makes absurd mistakes when it is new and untrained. The "oaths" and ceremonies and much of the boodling of the St. Louis ring seemed laughable to my corrupt friends in Philadelphia and Tammany Hall, and New York's own Tweed régime was "no joke," only because it was so general, and so expensive—to New York. It took time to perfect the "Philadelphia plan" of misgovernment, and it took time to educate Croker and develop his Tammany Hall. It will take time to evolve masters of the (in America) unstudied art of municipal government—time and demand. So far there has been no market for municipal experts in this country. All we are clamoring for today in our meek, weak-hearted way, is that mean, rudimentary virtue miscalled "common honesty." Do we really want it? Certainly Mayor Low is pecuniarily honest. He is more; he is conscientious and experienced and personally efficient. Bred to business, he rose above it, adding to the training he acquired in the conduct of an international commercial house, two terms as mayor of

Brooklyn, and to that again a very effective administration, as president, of the business of Columbia University. He began his mayoralty with a study of the affairs of New York; he has said himself that he devoted eight months to its finances: and he mastered this department and is admitted to be the master in detail of every department which has engaged his attention. In other words, Mr. Low has learned the business of New York; he is just about competent now to become the mayor of a great city. Is there a demand for Mr. Low?

No. When I made my inquiries—before the lying had begun—the Fusion leaders of the anti-Tammany forces, who nominated Mr. Low, said they might renominate him. "Who else was there?" they asked. And they thought he "might" be re-elected. The alternative was Richard Croker or Charles F. Murphy, his man, for no matter who Tammany's candidate for mayor was, if Tammany won, Tammany's boss would rule. The personal issue was plain enough. Yet there was no assurance for Mr. Low.

Why? There are many forms of the answer given, but they nearly all reduce themselves to one—the man's personality. It is not very engaging. Mr. Low has many respectable qualities, but these never are amiable. "Did you ever see his smile?" said a politician who was trying to account for his instinctive dislike for the mayor. I had; there is no laughter back of it, no humor, and no sense thereof. The appealing human element is lacking all through. His good abilities are self-sufficient; his dignity is smug; his courtesy seems not kind; his self-reliance is called obstinacy because, though he listens, he seems not to care; though he understands, he shows no sympathy, and when he decides, his reasoning is private. His most useful virtues—probity, intelligence, and conscientiousness—in action are often an irritation; they are so contented. Mr. Low is the bourgeois reformer type. Even where he compromises he gets no credit; his concessions make the impression of surrenders. A politician can say "no" and make a friend, where Mr. Low will lose one by saying "yes." Cold and impersonal, he cools even his heads of departments. Loyal public service they give, because his taste is for men who would do their duty for their own sake, not for his, and that excellent service the city has had. But members of Mr. Low's administration helped me to characterize him; they could not help it. Mr. Low's is not a lovable character.

But what of that? Why should his colleagues love him? Why should anybody like him? Why should he seek to charm, win affection, and make friends? He was elected to attend to the business of his office and to appoint subordinates who should attend to the business of their offices, not to make "political strength" and win elections. William Travers Jerome, the picturesque District Attorney, whose sincerity and intellectual honesty made sure the election of Mr. Low two years ago, detests him as a bourgeois, but the mayoralty is held in New York to be a bourgeois office. Mr. Low is the ideal product of the New York theory that municipal government is business, not politics, and that a business man who would manage the city as he would a business corporation, would solve for us all our troubles. Chicago reformers think we have got to solve our own problems; that government is political business; that men brought up in politics and experienced in public office will make the best administrators. They have refused to turn from their politician mayor, Carter H. Harrison, for the most ideal business candidate, and I have heard them say that when Chicago was ripe for a better mayor they would prefer a candidate chosen from among their well-tried aldermen. Again, I say, however, that this is only one way, and New York has another, and this other is the standard American way.

But again I say, also, that the New York way is on trial, for New York has what the whole country has been looking for in all municipal crises—the non-political ruler. Mr. Low's very faults, which I have emphasized for the purpose, emphasize the point. They make it impossible for him to be a politician even if he should wish to be. As for his selfishness, his lack of tact, his coldness—these are of no consequence. He has done his duty all the better for them. Admit that he is uninteresting; what does that matter? He has served the city. Will the city not vote for him because it does not like the way he smiles? Absurd as it sounds, that is what all I have heard against Low amounts to. But to reduce the situation to a further absurdity, let us eliminate altogether the personality of Mr. Low. Let us suppose he has no smile, no courtesy, no dignity, no efficiency, no personality at all; suppose he were an It and had not given New York a good administration, but had only honestly tried. What then?

Tammany Hall? That is the alternative. The Tammany politicians see it just as clear as that, and they are not in the habit of deceiving themselves. They say "it is a Tammany year," "Tammany's turn." They say it and they believe it. They study the people, and they know it is all a matter of citizenship; they admit that they cannot win unless a goodly part of the independent vote goes to them; and still they say they can beat Mr. Low or any other man the anti-Tammany forces may nominate. So we are safe in eliminating Mr. Low and reducing the issue to plain Tammany.

Tammany is bad government; not inefficient, but dishonest; not a party, not a delusion and a snare, hardly known by its party name—Democracy; having little standing in the national councils of the party and caring little for influence outside of the city. Tammany is Tammany, the embodiment of corruption. All the world knows and all the world may know what it is and what it is after. For hypocrisy is not a Tammany vice. Tammany is for Tammany, and the Tammany men say so. Other rings proclaim lies and make pretensions; other rogues talk about the tariff and imperialism. Tammany is honestly dishonest. Time and time again, in private and in public, the leaders, big and little, have said they are out for themselves and their own; not for the public, but for "me and my friends"; not for New York, but for Tammany. Richard Croker said under oath once that he worked for his own pockets all the time, and Tom Grady, the Tammany orator, has brought his crowds to their feet cheering sentiments as primitive, stated with candor as brutal.

The man from Mars would say that such an organization, so self-confessed, could not be very dangerous to an intelligent people. Foreigners marvel at it and at us, and even Americans—Pennsylvanians, for example—cannot understand why we New Yorkers regard Tammany as so formidable. I think I can explain it. Tammany is corruption with consent; it is bad government founded on the suffrages of the people. The Philadelphia machine is more powerful. It rules Philadelphia by fraud and force and does not require the votes of the people. The Philadelphians do not vote for their machine; their machine votes for them. Tammany used to stuff the ballot boxes and intimidate voters; to-day there is practically none of that.

Tammany rules, when it rules, by right of the votes of the people of New York.

Tammany corruption is democratic corruption. That of the Philadelphia ring is rooted in special interests. Tammany, too, is allied with "vested interests"—but Tammany labors under disadvantages not known in Philadelphia. The Philadelphia ring is of the same party that rules the State and the nation, and the local ring forms a living chain with the State and national rings. Tammany is a purely local concern. With a majority only in old New York, it has not only to buy what it wants from the Republican majority in the State, but must trade to get the whole city. Big business everywhere is the chief source of political corruption, and it is one source in New York; but most of the big businesses represented in New York have no plants there. Offices there are, and head offices, of many trusts and railways, for example, but that is all. There are but two railway terminals in the city, and but three railways use them. These have to do more with Albany than New York. So with Wall Street. Philadelphia's stock exchange deals largely in Pennsylvania securities, New York's in those of the whole United States. There is a small Wall Street group that specializes in local corporations, and they are active and give Tammany a Wall Street connection, but the biggest and the majority of our financial leaders, bribers though they may be in other cities and even in New York State, are independent of Tammany Hall, and can be honest citizens at home. From this class, indeed, New York can, and often does, draw some of its reformers. Not so Philadelphia. That bourgeois opposition which has persisted for thirty years in the fight against Tammany corruption was squelched in Philadelphia after its first great uprising. Matt Quay, through the banks, railways, and other business interests, was able to reach it. A large part of his power is negative; there is no opposition. Tammany's power is positive. Tammany cannot reach all the largest interests and its hold is upon the people.

Tammany's democratic corruption rests upon the corruption of the people, the plain people, and there lies its great significance; its grafting system is one in which more individuals share than any I have studied. The people themselves get very little; they come cheap, but they are interested. Divided into districts, the organization subdivides them into precincts or neighborhoods, and their sovereign power, in the form of votes, is bought up by kindness and petty privileges. They are forced to a surrender, when necessary, by intimidation, but the leader and his captains have their hold because they take care of their own. They speak pleasant words, smile friendly smiles, notice the baby, give picnics up the River or the Sound, or a slap on the back; find jobs, most of them at the city's expense, but they have also newsstands, peddling privileges, railroad and other business places to dispense; they permit violations of the law, and, if a man has broken the law without permission, see him through the court. Though a blow in the face is as readily given as a shake of the hand, Tammany kindness is real kindness, and will go far, remember long, and take infinite trouble for a friend.

The power that is gathered up thus cheaply, like garbage, in the districts is concentrated in the district leader, who in turn passes it on through a general committee to the boss. This is a form of living government, extra-legal, but very actual, and, though the beginnings of it are purely democratic, it develops at each stage into an autocracy. In Philadelphia the boss appoints a district leader and gives him power. Tammany has done that in two or three notable instances, but never without causing a bitter fight which lasts often for years. In Philadelphia the State boss designates the city boss. In New York, Croker has failed signally to maintain vice-bosses whom he appointed. The boss of Tammany Hall is a growth, and just as Croker grew, so has Charles F. Murphy grown up to Croker's place. Again, whereas in Philadelphia the boss and his ring handle and keep almost all of the graft, leaving little to the district leaders, in New York the district leaders share handsomely in the spoils.

There is more to share in New York. It is impossible to estimate the amount of it, not only for me, but for anybody. No Tammany man knows it all. Police friends of mine say that the Tammany leaders never knew how rich police corruption was till the Lexow committee exposed it, and that the politicians who had been content with small presents, contributions, and influence, "did not butt in" for their share till they saw by the testimony of frightened police grafters that the department was worth from four to five millions a year. The items are so incredible that I hesitate to print them. Devery told a friend once that in one year the police graft was "something over $3,000,000." Afterward the syndicate which divided the graft under Devery took in for thirty-six months $400,000 a month from gambling and poolrooms alone. Saloon bribers, disorderly house blackmail, policy, etc., etc., bring this total up to amazing proportions.

Yet this was but one department, and a department that was overlooked by Tammany for years. The annual budget of the city is about $100,000,000, and though the power that comes of the expenditure of that amount is enormous and the opportunities for rake-offs infinite, this sum is not one-half of the resources of Tammany when it is in power. Her resources are the resources of the city as a business, as a political, as a social power. If Tammany could be incorporated, and all its earnings, both legitimate and illegitimate, gathered up and paid over in dividends, the stockholders would get more than the New York Central bond- and stockholders, more than the Standard Oil stockholders, and the controlling clique would wield a power equal to that of the United States Steel Company. Tammany, when in control of New York, takes out of the city unbelievable millions of dollars a year.

No wonder the leaders are all rich; no wonder so many more Tammany men are rich than are the leaders in any other town; no wonder Tammany is liberal in its division of the graft. Croker took the best and the safest of it, and he accepted shares in others. He was "in on the Wall Street end," and the Tammany clique of financiers have knocked down and bought up at low prices Manhattan Railway stock by threats of the city's power over the road; they have been let in on Metropolitan deals and on the Third Avenue Railroad grab; the Ice trust is a Tammany trust; they have banks and trust companies, and through the New York Realty Company are forcing alliances with such financial groups as that of the Standard Oil Company. Croker shared in these deals and businesses. He sold judgeships, taking his pay in the form of contributions to the Tammany campaign fund, of which he was treasurer, and he had the judges take from the regular real estate exchange all the enormous real estate business that passed through the courts, and give it to an exchange connected with the real estate business of his firm, Peter F. Meyer & Co. This alone would maintain a ducal estate in England. But his real estate business was greater than that. It had extraordinary legal facilities, the free advertising of abuse, the prestige of political privilege, all of which brought in trade; and it had advance information and followed, with profitable deals, great public improvements.

Though Croker said he worked for his own pockets all the time, and did take the best of the graft, he was not "hoggish." Some of the richest graft in the city is in the Department of Buildings: $100,000,000 a year goes into building operations in New York. All of this, from outhouses to sky-scrapers, is subject to very precise laws and regulations, most of them wise, some impossible. The Building Department has the enforcement of these; it passes upon all construction, private and public, at all stages, from plan-making to actual completion; and can cause not only "unavoidable delay," but can wink at most profitable violations. Architects and builders had to stand in with the department. They called on the right man and they settled on a scale which was not fixed, but which generally was on the basis of the department's estimate of a fair half of the value of the saving in time or bad material. This brought in at least a banker's percentage on one hundred millions a year. Croker, so far as I can make out, took none of this! it was let out to other leaders and was their own graft.

District Attorney William Travers Jerome has looked into the Dock Department, and he knows things which he yet may prove. This is an important investigation for two reasons. It is very large graft, and the new Tammany leader, Charlie Murphy, had it. New York wants to know more about Murphy, and it should want to know about the management of its docks, since, just as other cities have their corrupt dealings with railways and their terminals, so New York's great terminal business is with steamships and docks. These docks should pay the city handsomely. Mr. Murphy says they shouldn't; he is wise, as Croker was before he became old and garrulous, and, as Tammany men put it, "keeps his mouth shut," but he did say that the docks should not be run for revenue to the city, but for their own improvement. The Dock Board has exclusive and private and secret control of the expenditure of $10,000,000 a year. No wonder Murphy chose it.

It is impossible to follow all New York graft from its source to its final destination. It is impossible to follow here the course of that which is well known to New Yorkers. There are public works for Tammany contractors. There are private works for Tammany contractors, and corporations and individuals find it expedient to let it go to Tammany contractors. Tammany has a very good system of grafting on public works; I mean that it is "good" from the criminal point of view—and so it has for the furnishing of supplies. Low bids and short deliveries, generally speaking (and that is the only way I can speak here), is the method. But the Tammany system, as a whole, is weak.

Tammany men as grafters have a confidence in their methods and system, which, in the light of such perfection as that of Philadelphia, is amusing, and the average New Yorker takes in "the organization" a queer sort of pride, which is ignorant and provincial. Tammany is 'way behind the times. It is growing; it has improved. In Tweed's day the politicians stole from the city treasury, divided the money on the steps of the City Hall, and, not only the leaders, big and little, but heelers and outsiders;

not only Tweed, but ward carpenters robbed the city; not only politicians, but newspapers and citizens were "in on the divvy." New York, not Tammany alone, was corrupt. When the exposure came, and Tweed asked his famous question, "What are you going to do about it?" the ring mayor, A. Oakey Hall, asked another as significant. It was reported that suit was to be brought against the ring to recover stolen funds. "Who is going to sue?" said Mayor Hall, who could not think of anybody of importance sufficiently without sin to throw the first stone. Stealing was stopped and grafting was made more businesslike, but still it was too general, and the boodling for the Broadway street railway franchise prompted a still closer grip on the business. The organization since then has been gradually concentrating the control of graft. Croker did not proceed so far along the line as the Philadelphia ring has, as the police scandals showed. After the Lexow exposures, Tammany took over that graft, but still let it go practically by districts, and the police captains still got a third. After the Mazet exposures, Devery became Chief, and the police graft was so concentrated that the division was reduced to fourteen parts. Again, later, it was reduced to a syndicate of four or five men, with a dribble of miscellaneous graft for the police. In Philadelphia the police have nothing to do with the police graft; a policeman may collect it, but he acts for a politician, who in turn passes it up to a small ring. That is the drift in New York. Under Devery the police officers got comparatively little, and the rank and file themselves were blackmailed for transfers and promotions, for remittances of fines, and in a dozen other petty ways.

Philadelphia is the end toward which New York under Tammany is driving as fast as the lower intelligence and higher conceit of its leaders will let it. In Philadelphia one very small ring gets everything, dividing the whole as it pleases, and not all those in the inner ring are politicians. Trusting few individuals, they are safe from exposure, more powerful, more deliberate, and they are wise as politicians. When, as in New York, the number of grafters is large, this delicate business is in some hands that are rapacious. The police grafters, for example, in Devery's day, were not content with the amounts collected from the big vices. They cultivated minor vices, like policy, to such an extent that the Policy King was caught and sent to prison, and Devery's wardman, Glennon, was pushed into so tight a hole that there was danger that District Attorney Jerome would get past Glennon to Devery and the syndicate. The murder of a witness the night he was in the Tenderloin police station served to save the day. But, worst of all, Tammany, the "friend of the people," permitted the organization of a band of so-called Cadets, who made a business, under the protection of the police, of ruining the daughters of the tenements and even of catching and imprisoning in disorderly houses the wives of poor men. This horrid traffic never was exposed; it could not and cannot be. Vicious women were "planted" in tenement houses and (I know this personally) the children of decent parents counted the customers, witnessed their transactions with these creatures, and, as a father told with shame and tears, reported totals at the family table.

Tammany leaders are usually the natural leaders of the people in these districts, and they are originally good-natured, kindly men. No one has a more sincere liking than I for some of those common but generous fellows; their charity is real, at first. But they sell out their own people. They do give them coal and help them in their private troubles, but, as they grow rich and powerful, the kindness goes out of the charity and they not only collect at their saloons or in rents—cash for their "goodness"; they not only ruin fathers and sons and cause the troubles they relieve; they sacrifice the children in the schools; let the Health Department neglect the tenements, and, worst of all, plant vice in the neighborhood and in the homes of the poor.

This is not only bad; it is bad politics; it has defeated Tammany. Woe to New York when Tammany learns better. Honest fools talk of the reform of Tammany Hall. It is an old hope, this, and twice it has been disappointed, but it is not vain. That is the real danger ahead. The reform of a corrupt ring means, as I have said before, the reform of its system of grafting and a wise consideration of certain features of good government. Croker turned his "best chief of police," William S. Devery, out of Tammany Hall, and, slow and old as he was, Croker learned what clean streets were from Colonel Waring, and gave them. Now there is a new boss, a young man, Charles F. Murphy, and unknown to New Yorkers. He looks dense, but he acts with force, decision, and skill. The new mayor will be his man. He may divide with Croker and leave to the "old man" all his accustomed graft, but Charlie Murphy will rule Tammany and, if Tammany is elected, New York also. Lewis Nixon is urging Murphy publicly, as I write, to declare against the police scandals and all the worst practices of Tammany. Lewis Nixon is an honest man, but he was one of the men Croker tried to appoint leader of Tammany Hall. And when he resigned Mr. Nixon said that he found that a man could not keep that leadership and his self-respect.

Yet Mr. Nixon is a type of the man who thinks Tammany would be fit to rule New York if the organization would "reform."

As a New Yorker, I fear Murphy will prove sagacious enough to do just that: stop the scandal, put all the graft in the hands of a few tried and true men, and give the city what it would call good government. Murphy says he will nominate for mayor a man so "good" that his goodness will astonish New York. I don't fear a bad Tammany mayor; I dread the election of a good one. For I have been to Philadelphia.

Philadelphia had a bad ring mayor, a man who promoted the graft and caused scandal after scandal. The leaders there, the wisest political grafters in this country, learned a great lesson from that. As one of them said to me:

"The American people don't mind grafting, but they hate scandals. They don't kick so much on a jiggered public contract for a boulevard, but they want the boulevard and no fuss and no dust. We want to give them that. We want to give them what they really want, a quiet Sabbath, safe streets, orderly nights, and homes secure. They let us have the police graft. But this mayor was a hog. You see, he had but one term and he could get his share only on what was made in his term. He not only took a hog's share off what was coming, but he wanted everything to come in his term. So I'm down on grafting mayors and grafting office holders. I tell you it's good politics to have honest men in office. I mean men that are personally honest."

So they got John Weaver for mayor, and honest John Weaver is checking corruption, restoring order, and doing a great many good things, which it is "good politics" to do. For he is satisfying the people, soothing their ruffled pride, and reconciling them to machine rule. I have letters from friends of mine there, honest men, who wish me to bear witness to the goodness of Mayor Weaver. I do. And I believe that if the Philadelphia machine leaders are as careful with Mayor Weaver as they have been and let him continue to give to the end as good government as he has given so far, the "Philadelphia plan" of graft will last and Philadelphia will never again be a free American city.

Philadelphia and New York began about the same time, some thirty years ago, to reform their city governments. Philadelphia got "good government"—what the Philadelphians call good—from a corrupt ring and quit, satisfied to be a scandal to the nation and a disgrace to democracy. New York has gone on fighting, advancing and retreating, for thirty years, till now it has achieved the beginnings, under Mayor Low, of a government for the people. Do the New Yorkers know it? Do they care? They are Americans, mixed and typical; do we Americans really want good government? Or, as I said at starting, have they worked for thirty years along the wrong road —crowded with unhappy American cities—the road to Philadelphia and despair?

Post Scriptum: Mayor Low was nominated on the Fusion ticket. Tammany nominated George B. McClellan. The local corporations contributed heavily to the Tammany campaign fund and the people of New York elected the Tammany ticket by a decisive majority of 62,696. The vote was: McClellan, 314,782; Low, 252,086.